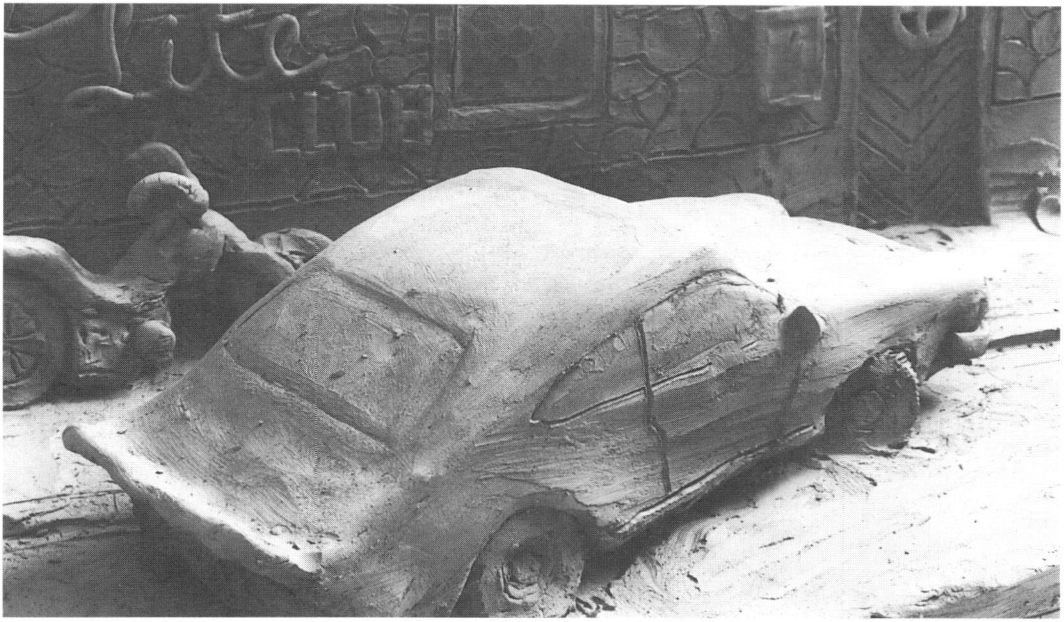

3 Hangout

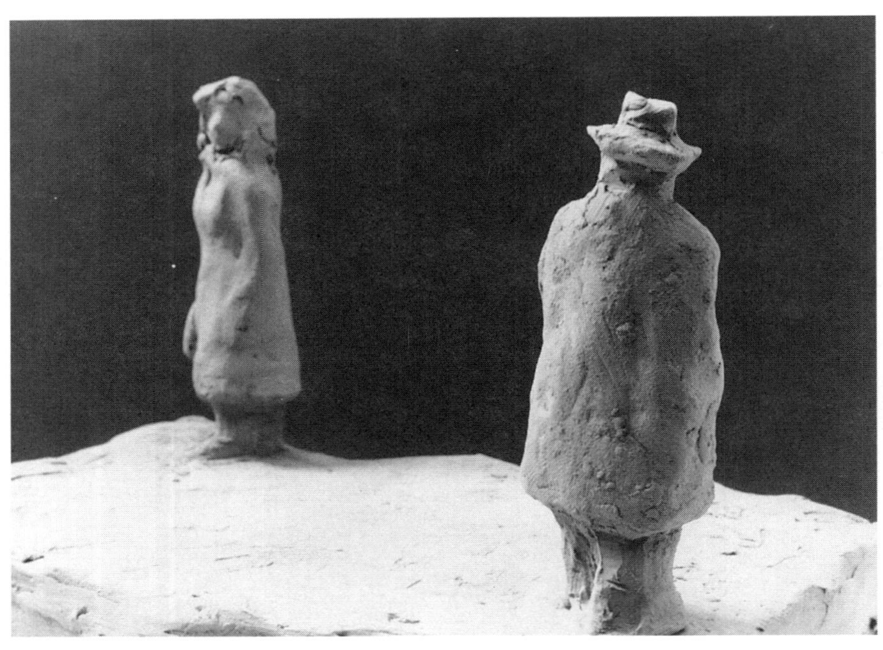

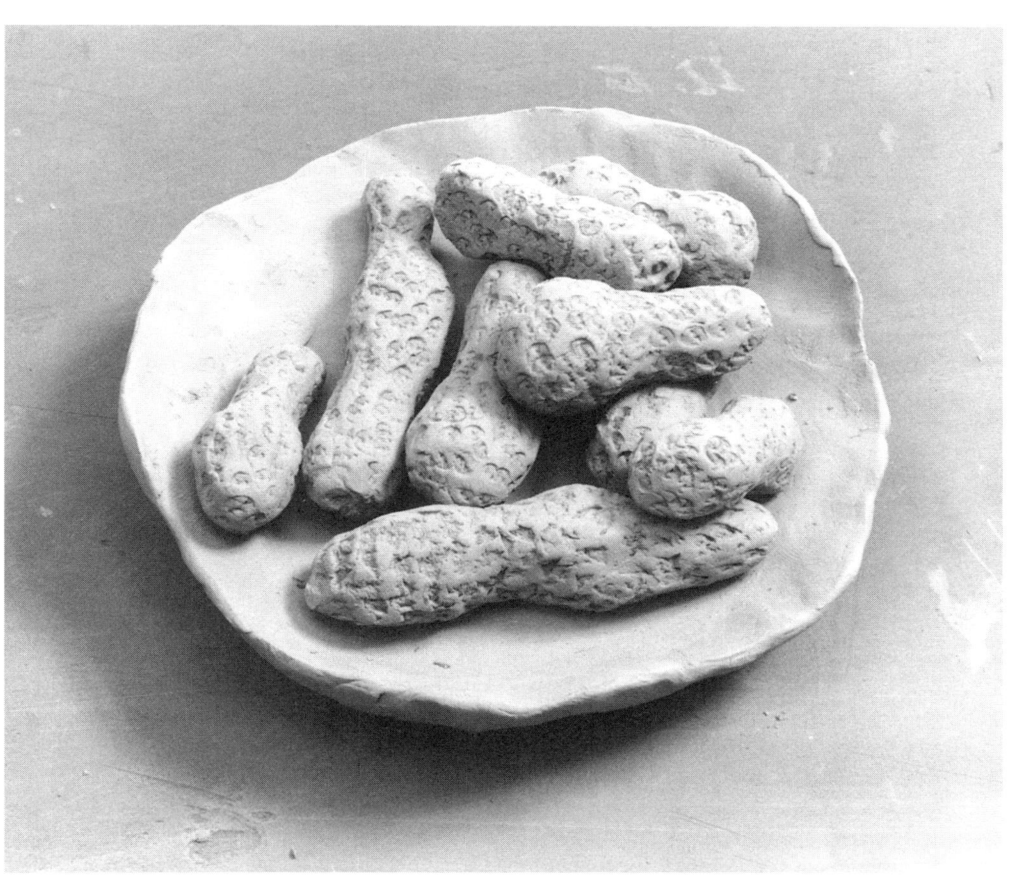

5   Peanuts

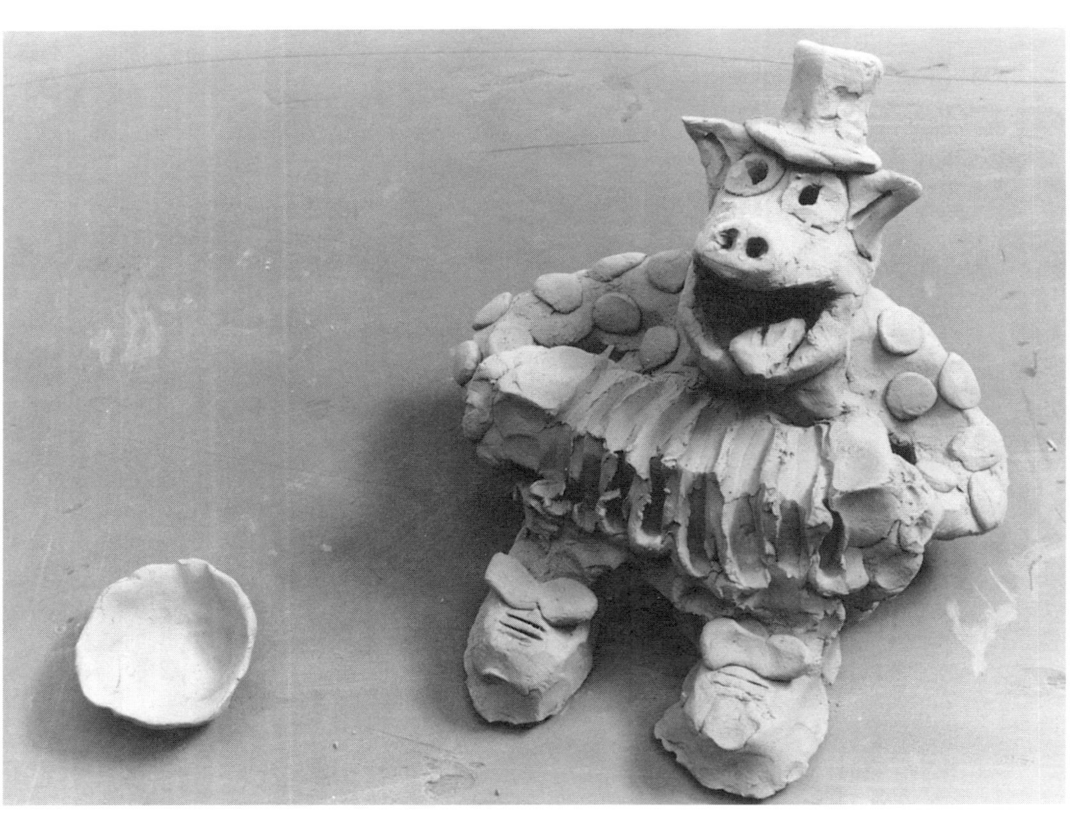

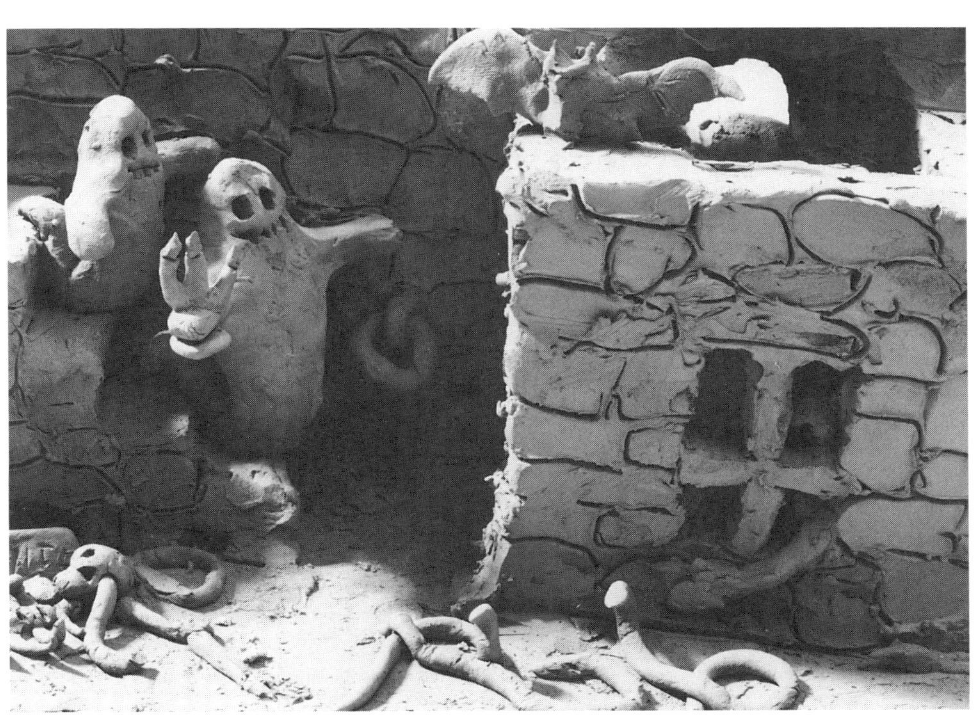

7   In the cellar

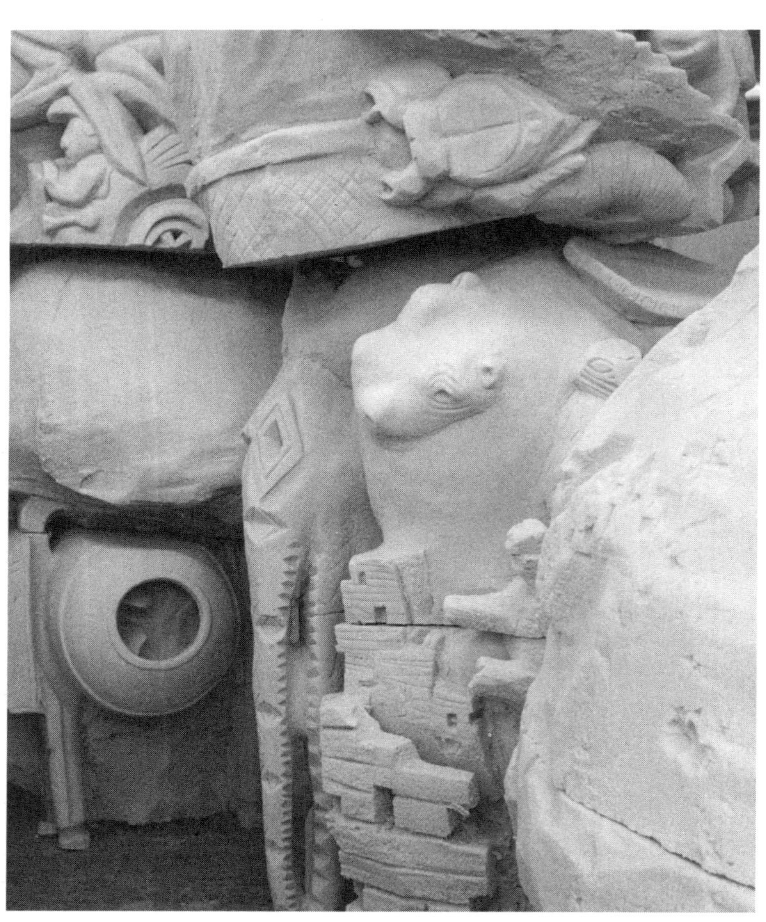

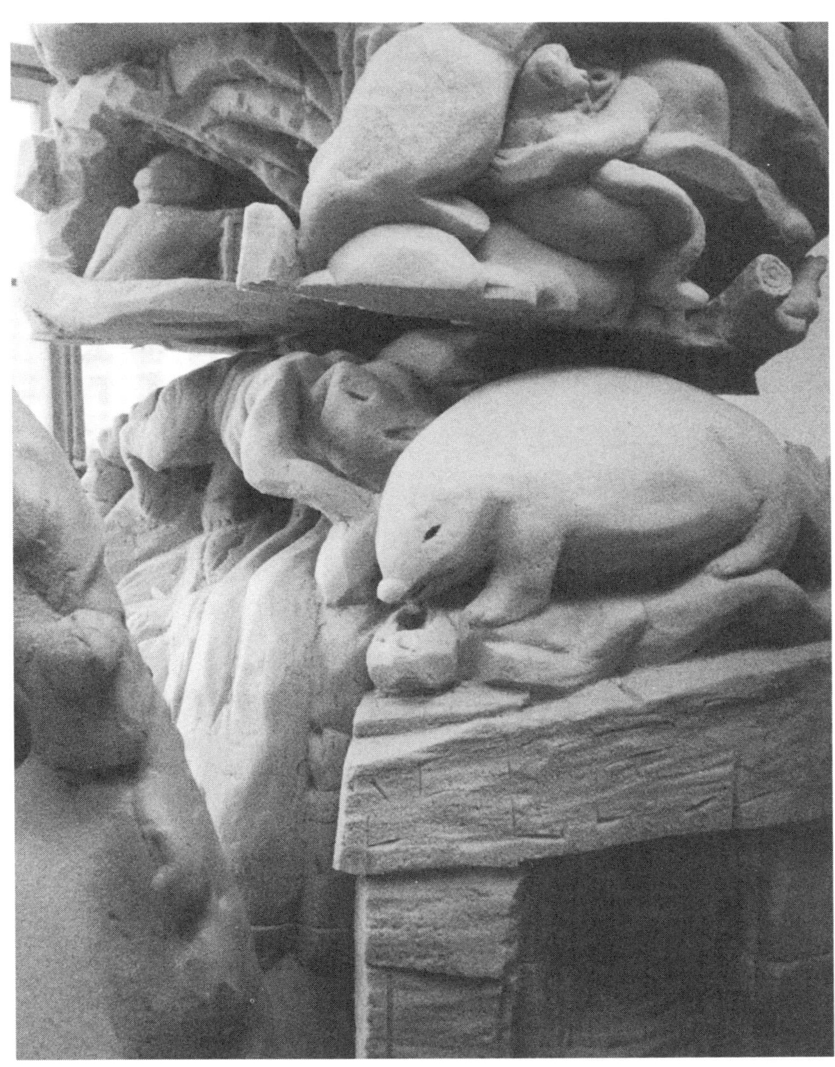

9 In the studio: Fever

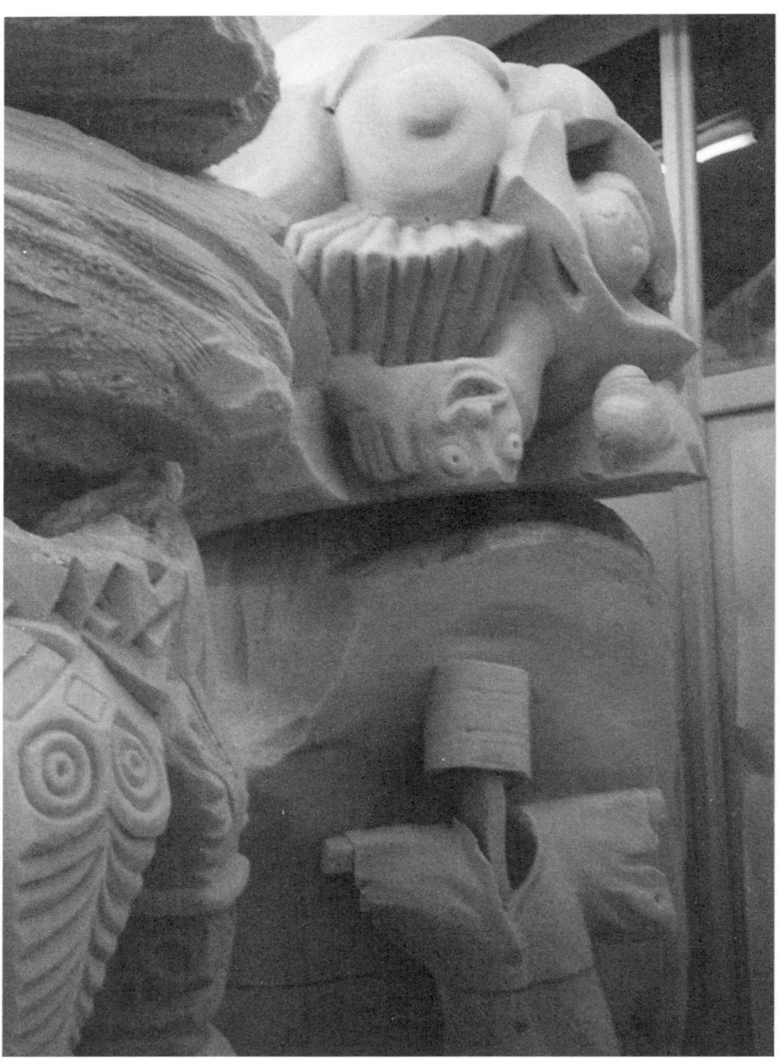

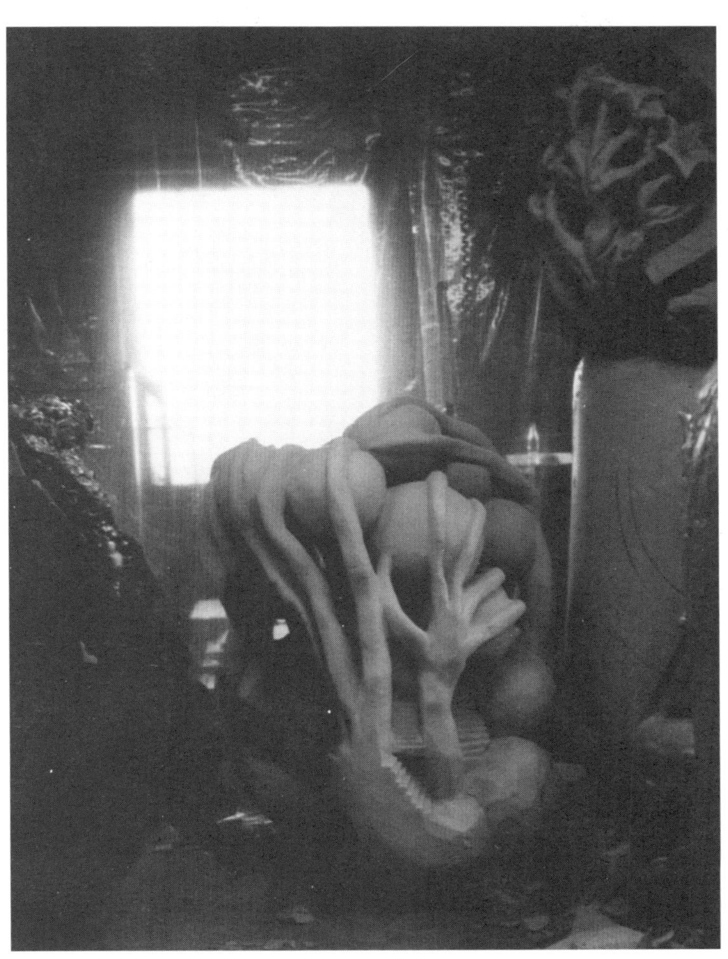

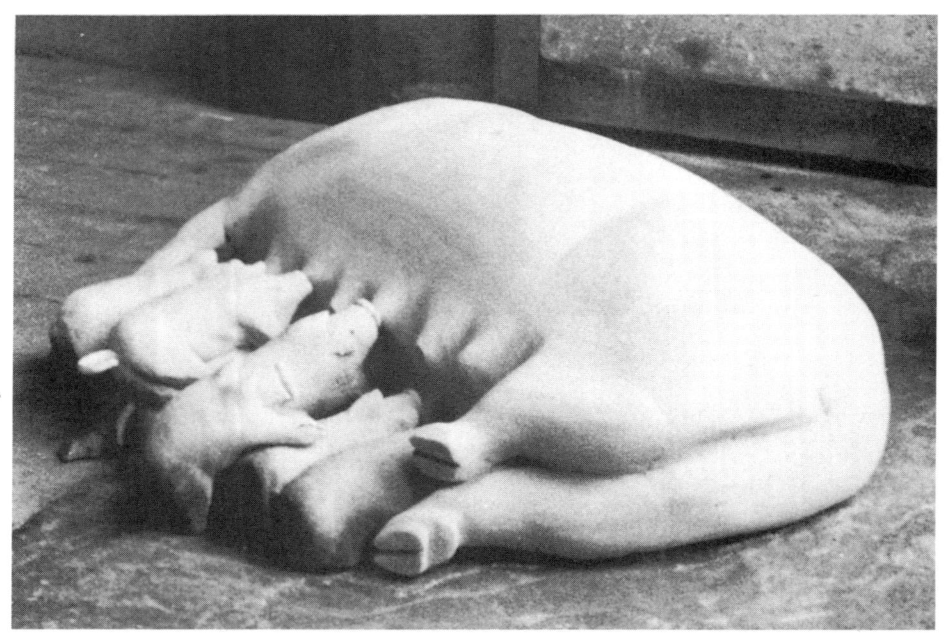

12   Pig and piglets

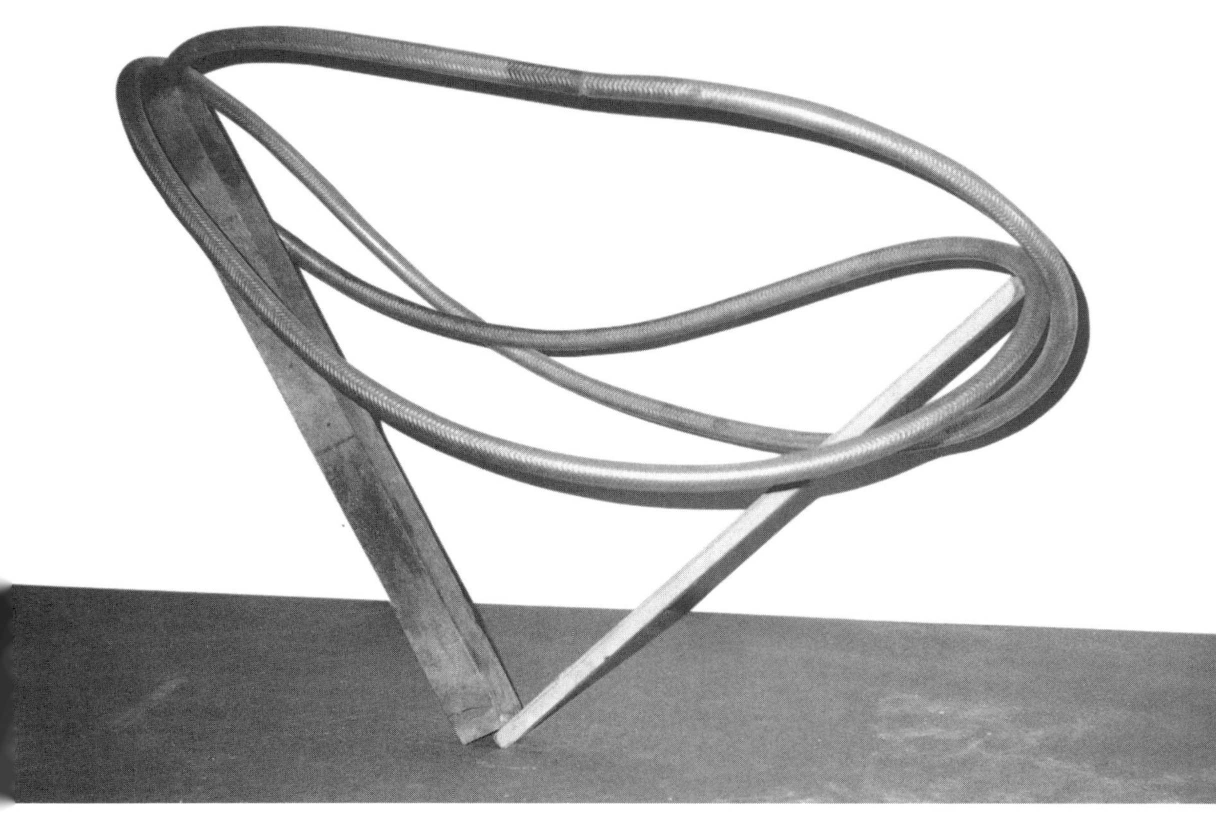

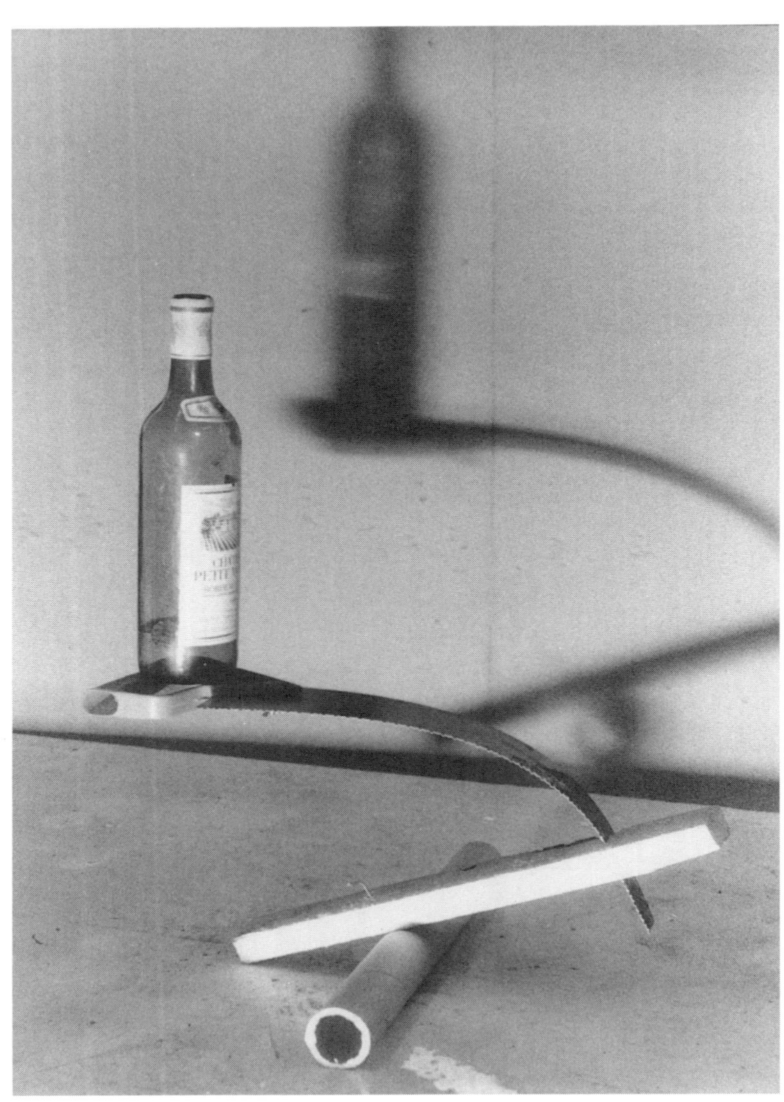

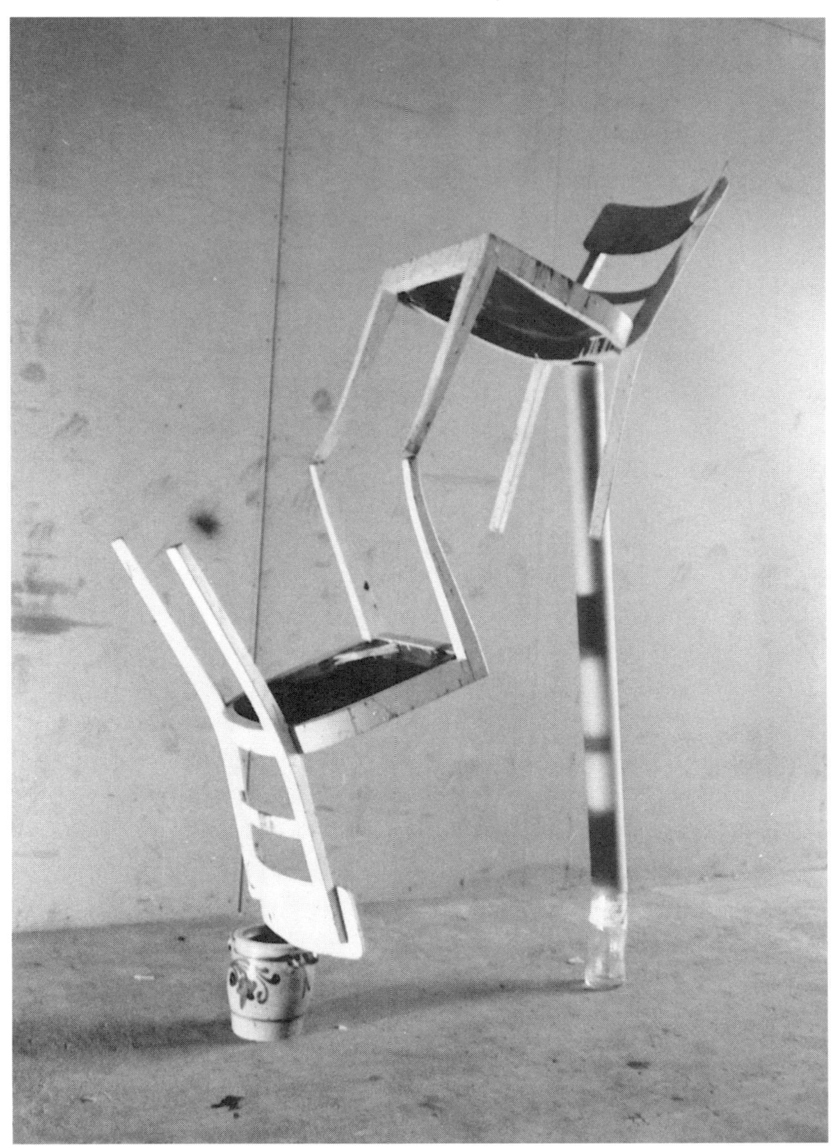

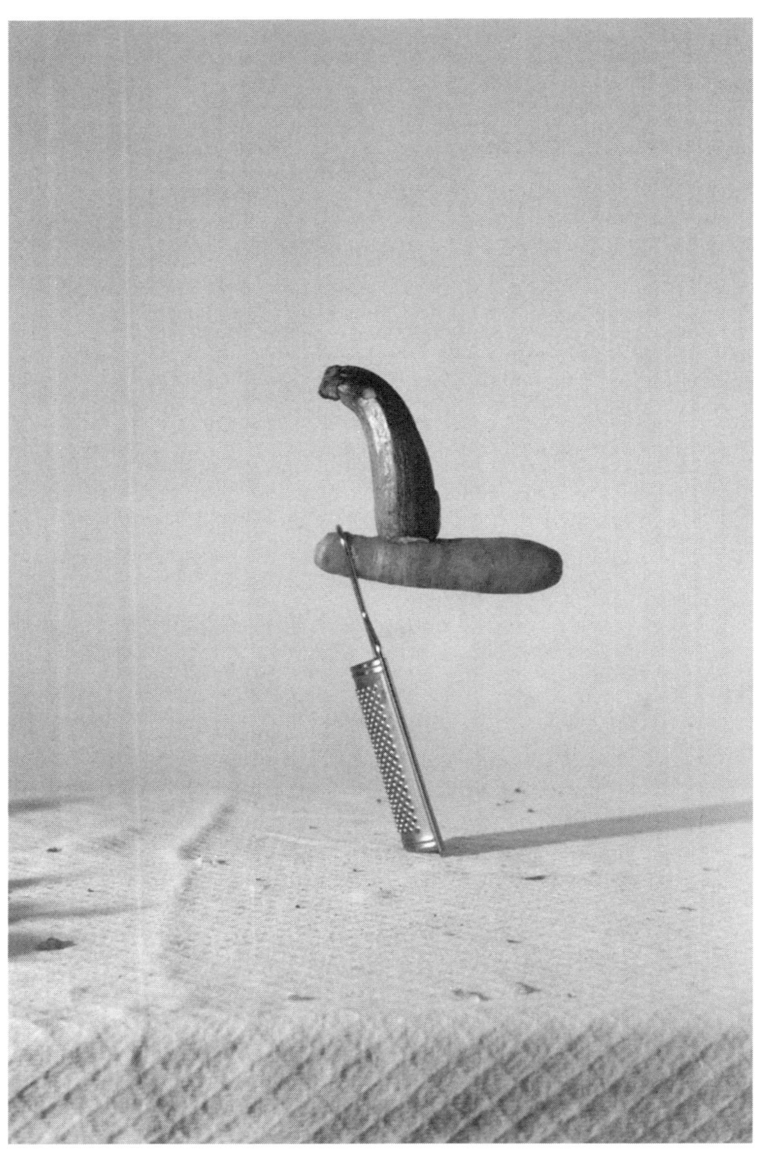

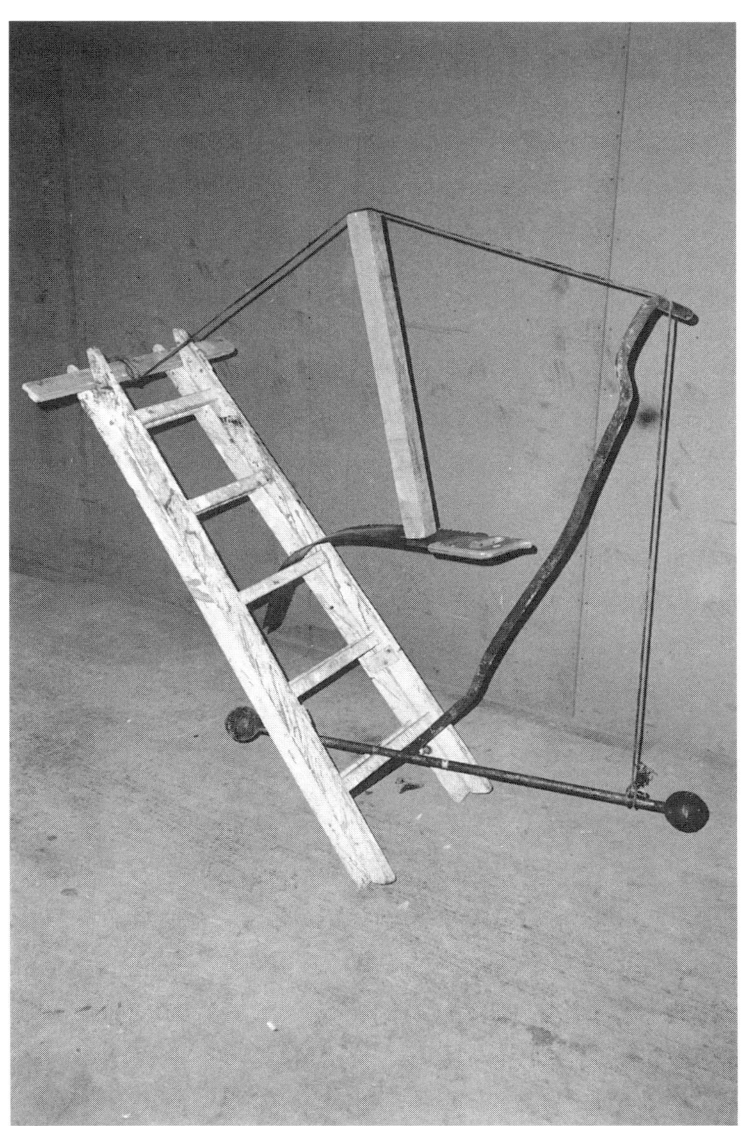

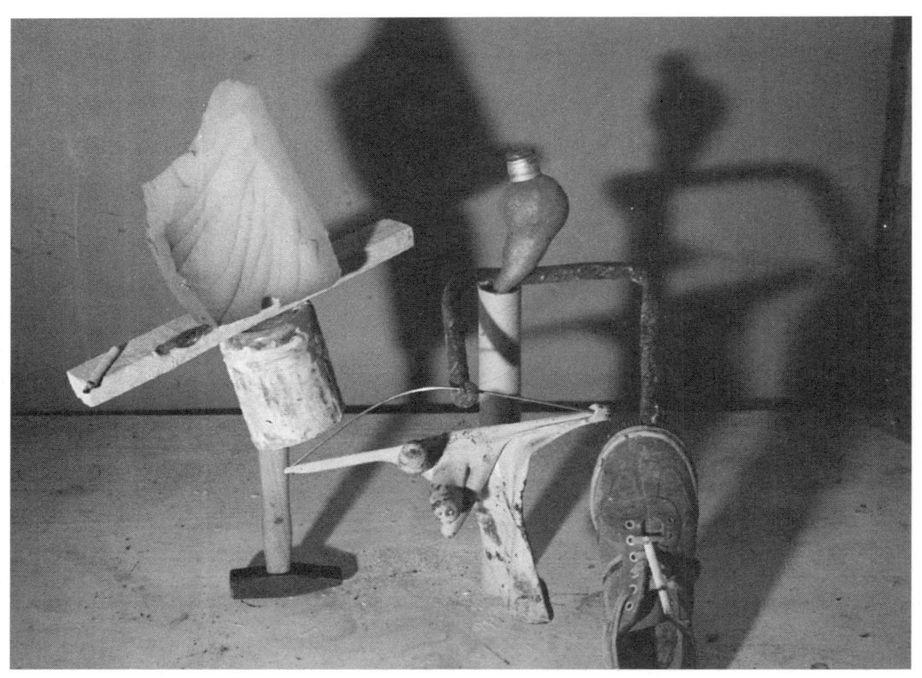

18   Mrs. Pear bringing her husband a freshly ironed shirt for the opera. The boy smokes.

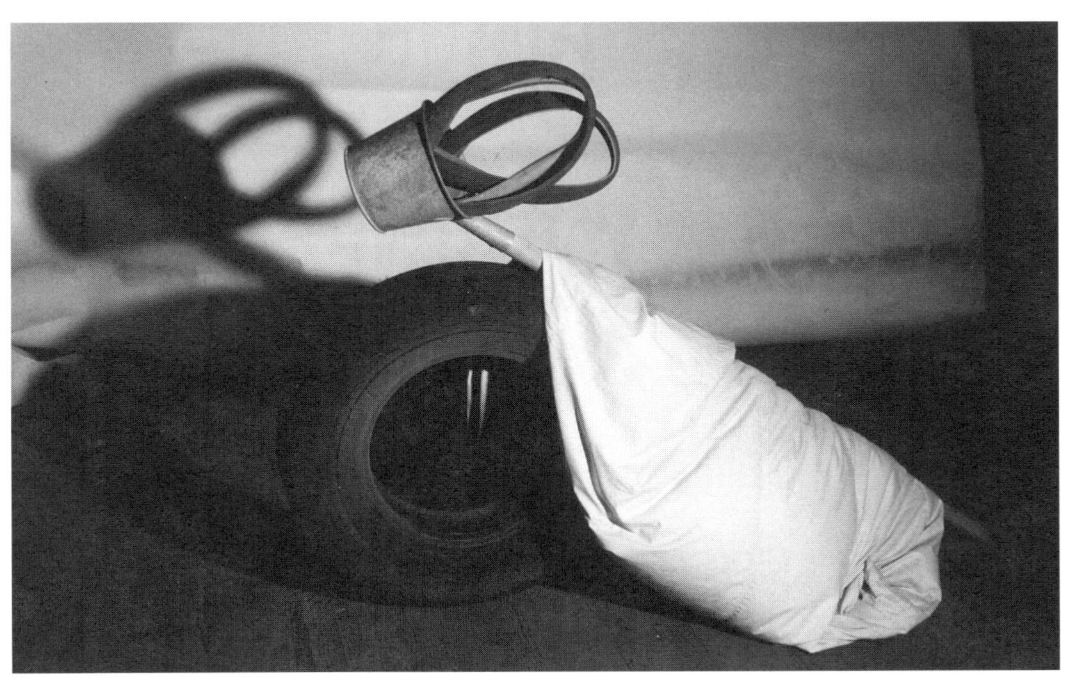

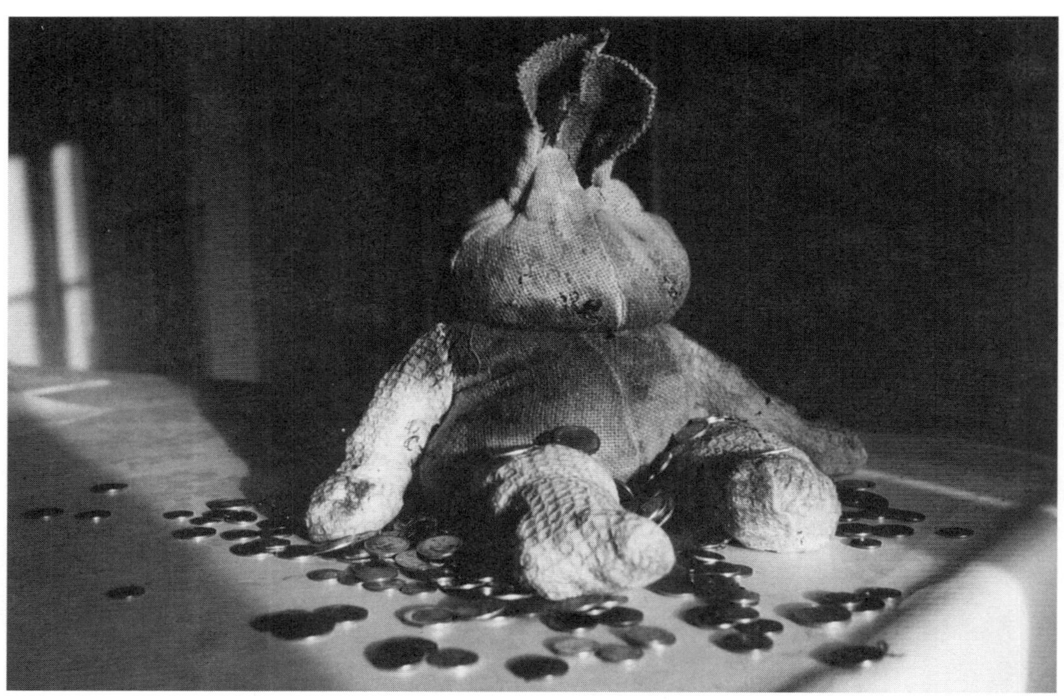

20   Cloth doll

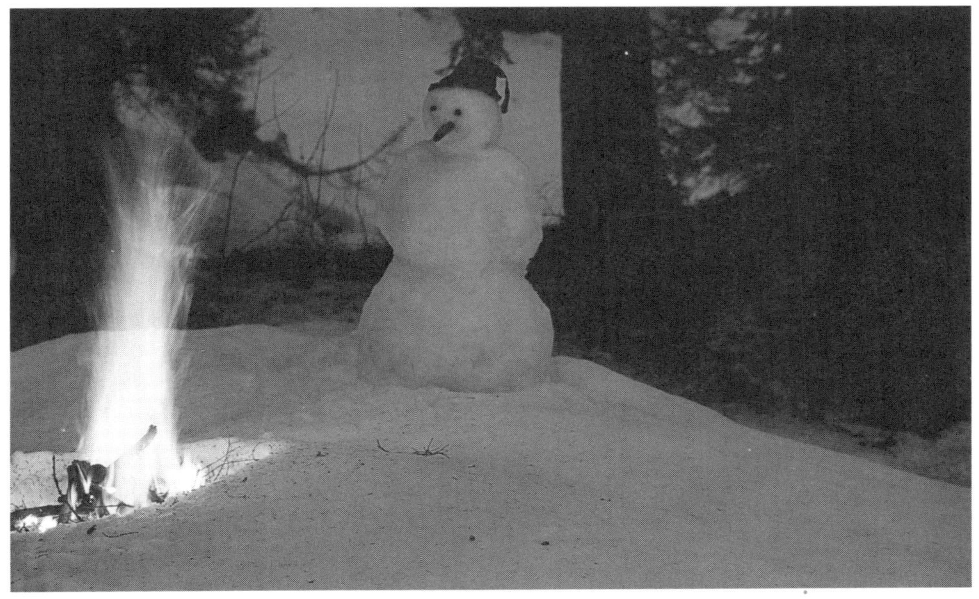

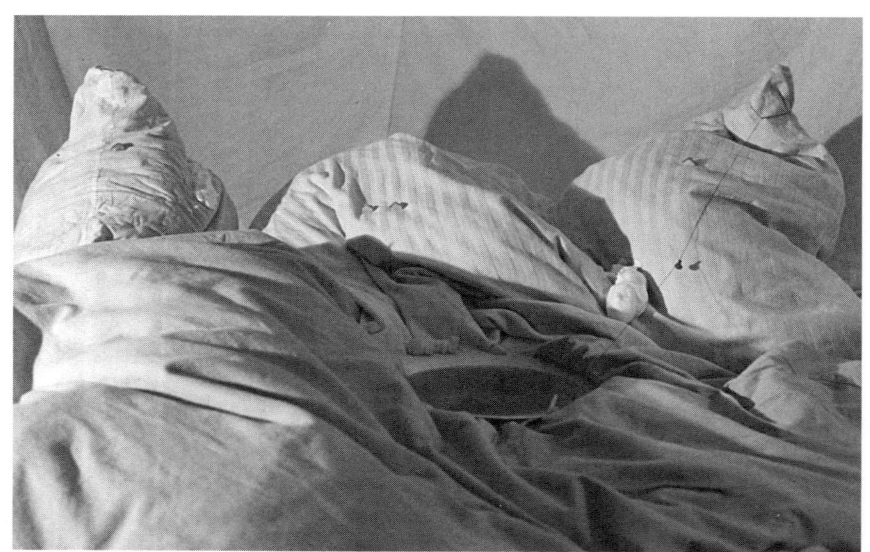

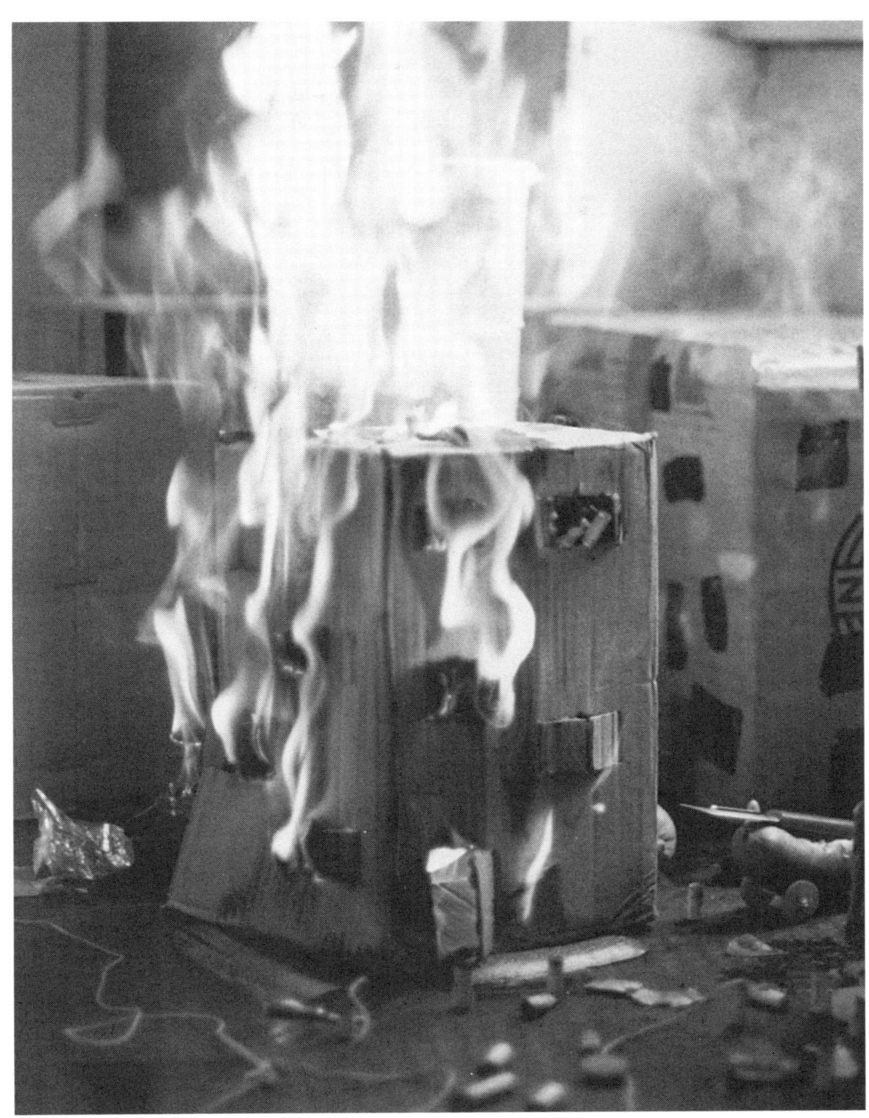

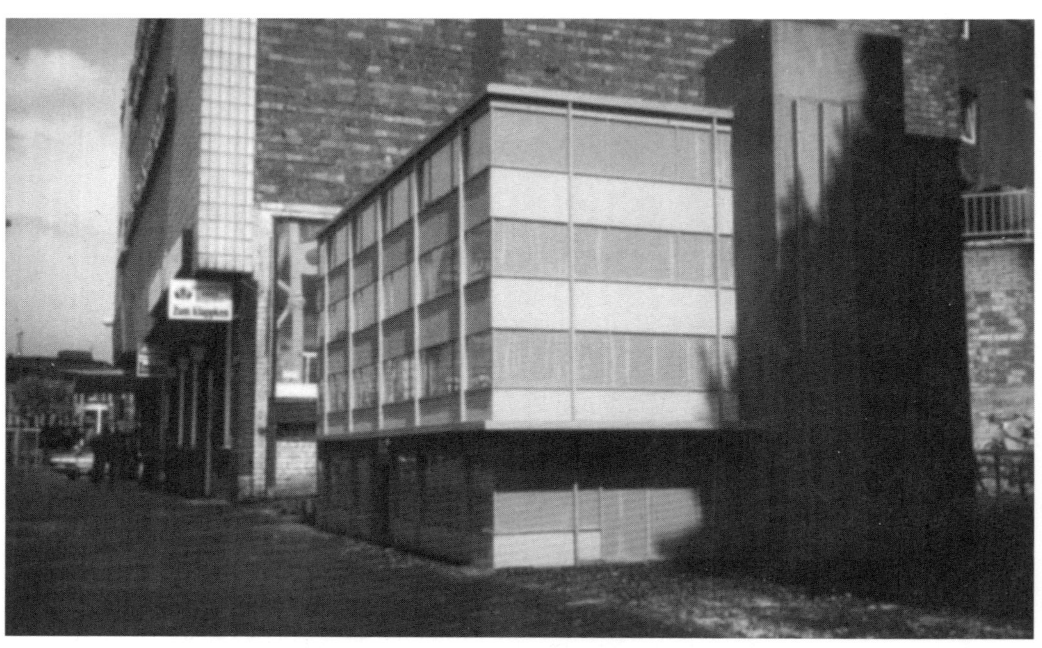

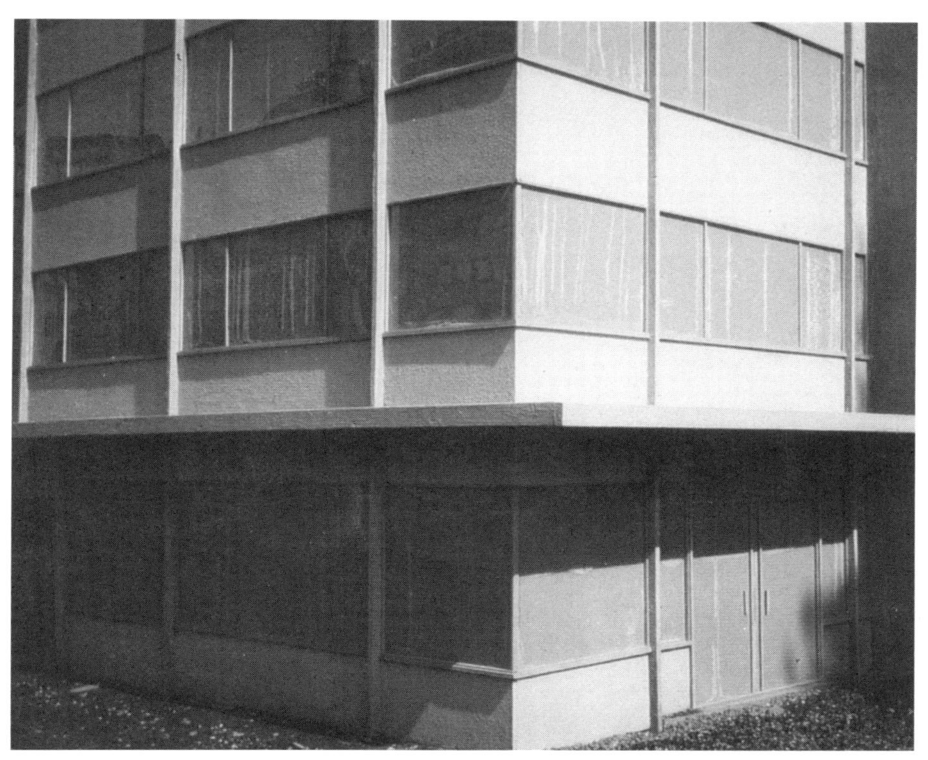

25 Corner

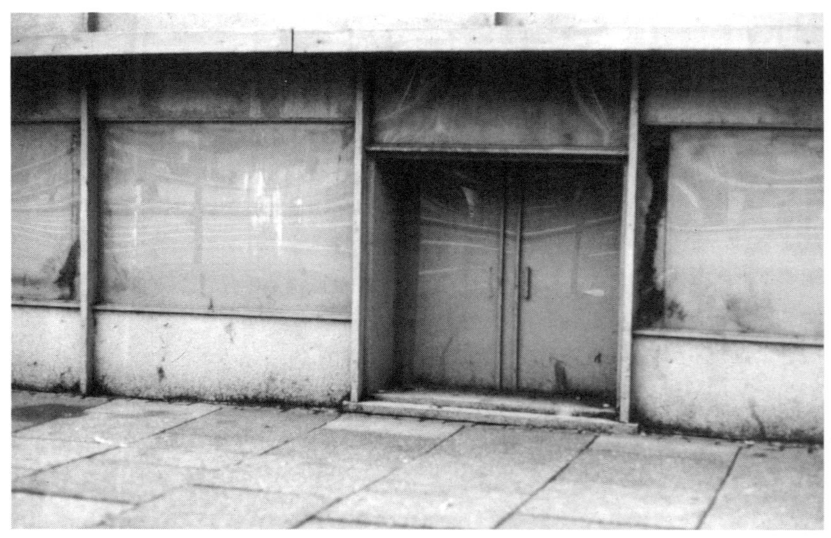

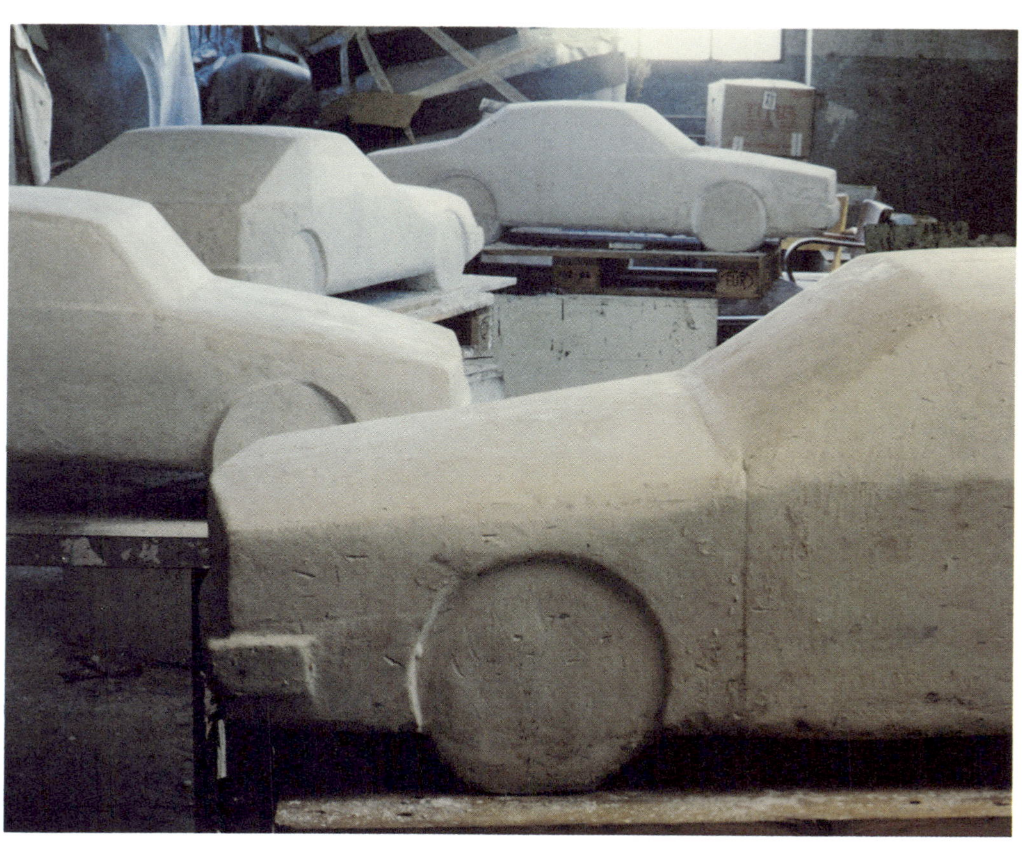

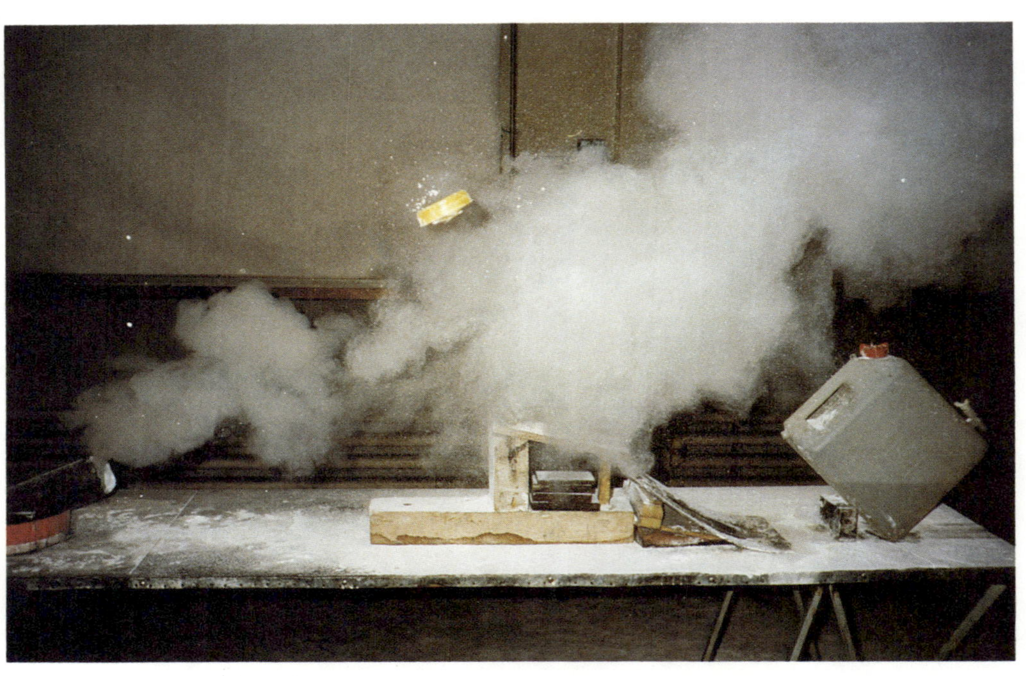

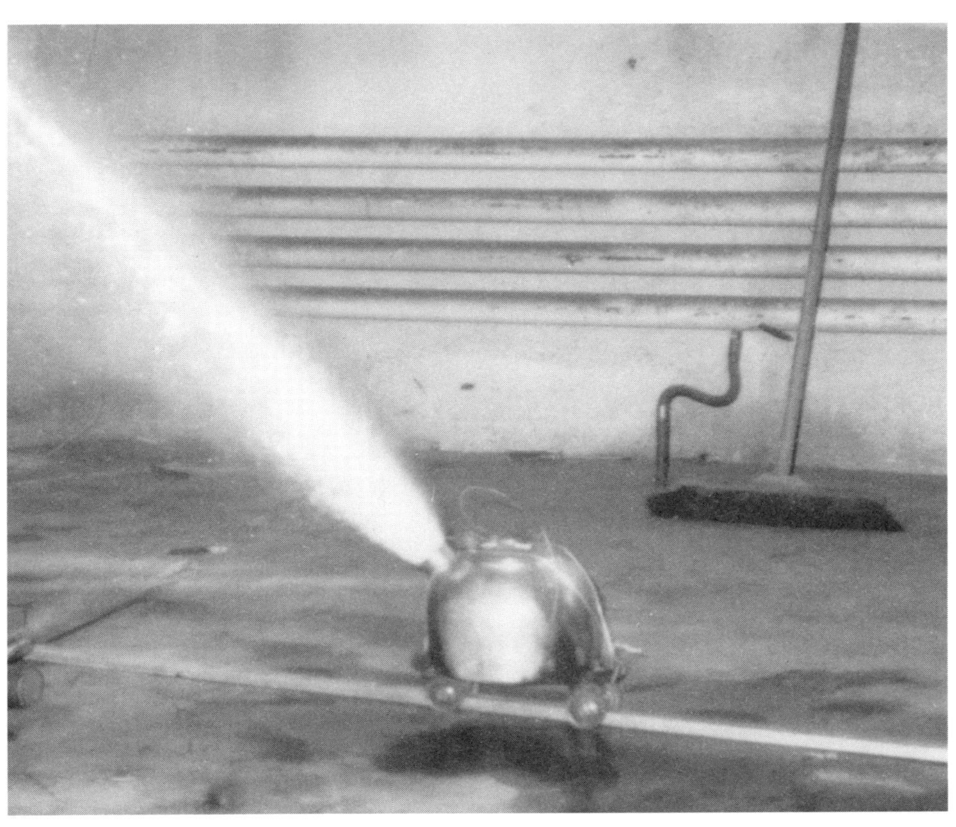

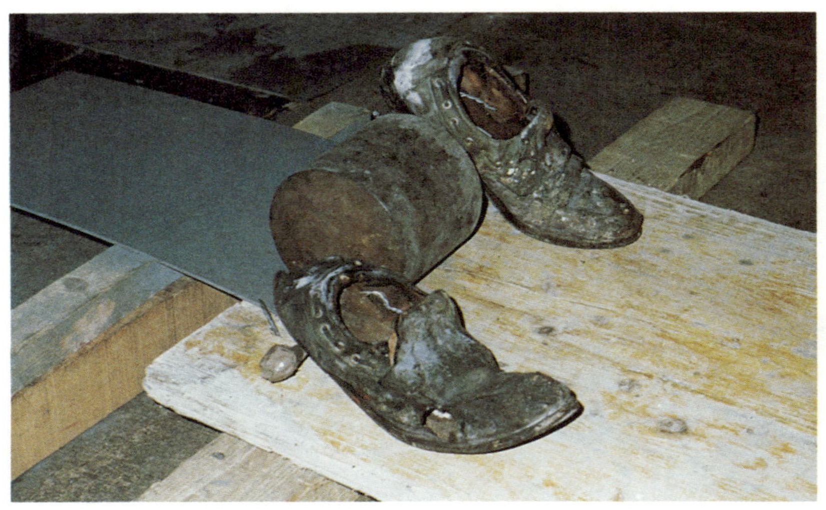

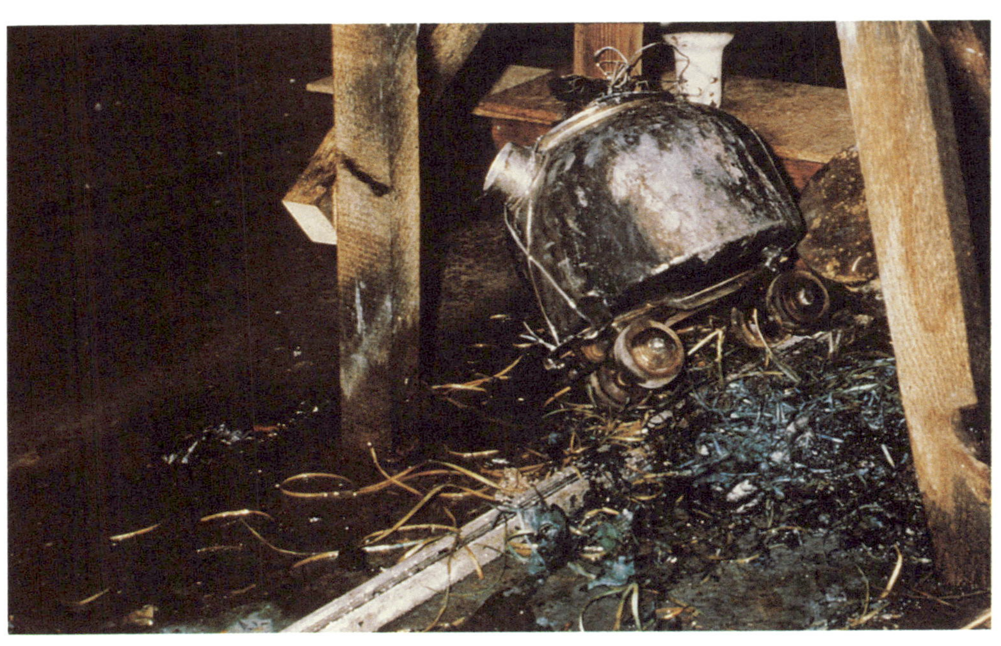

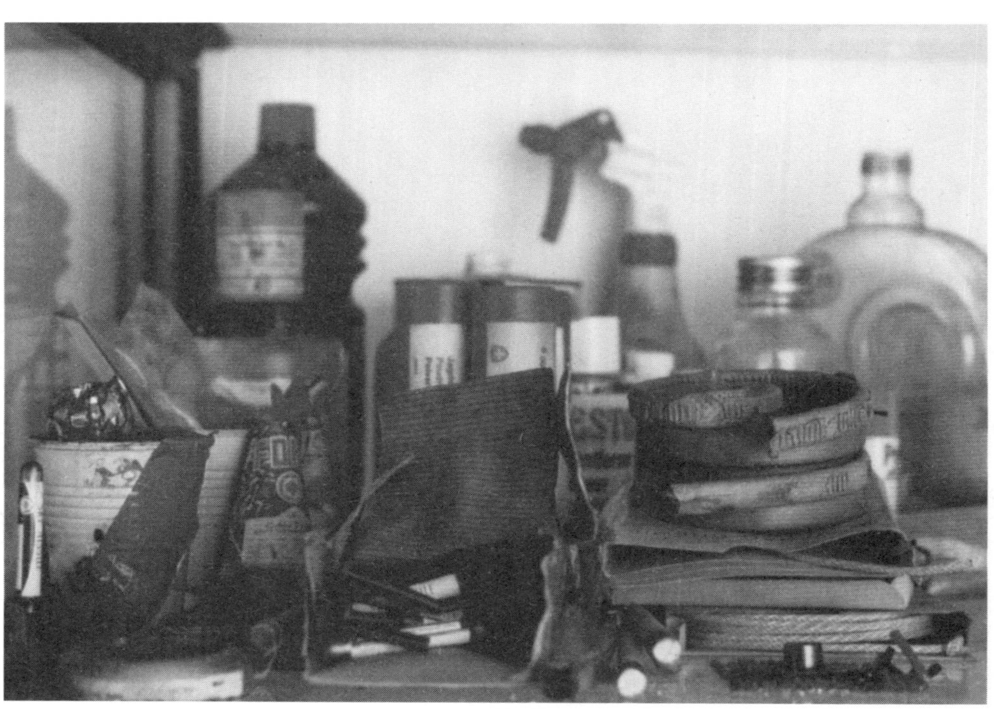

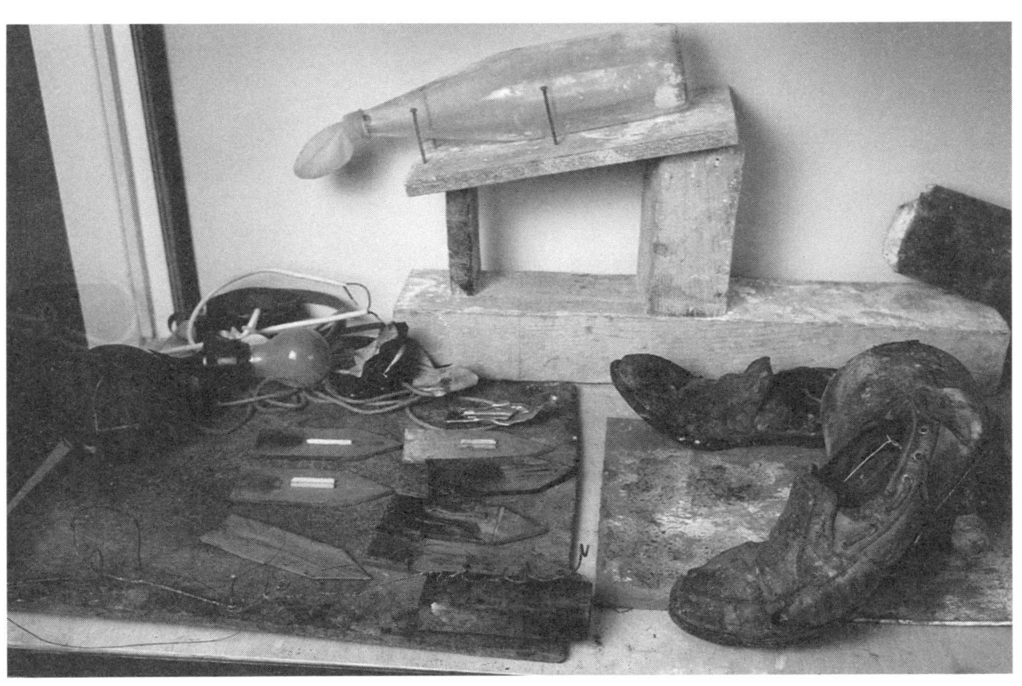

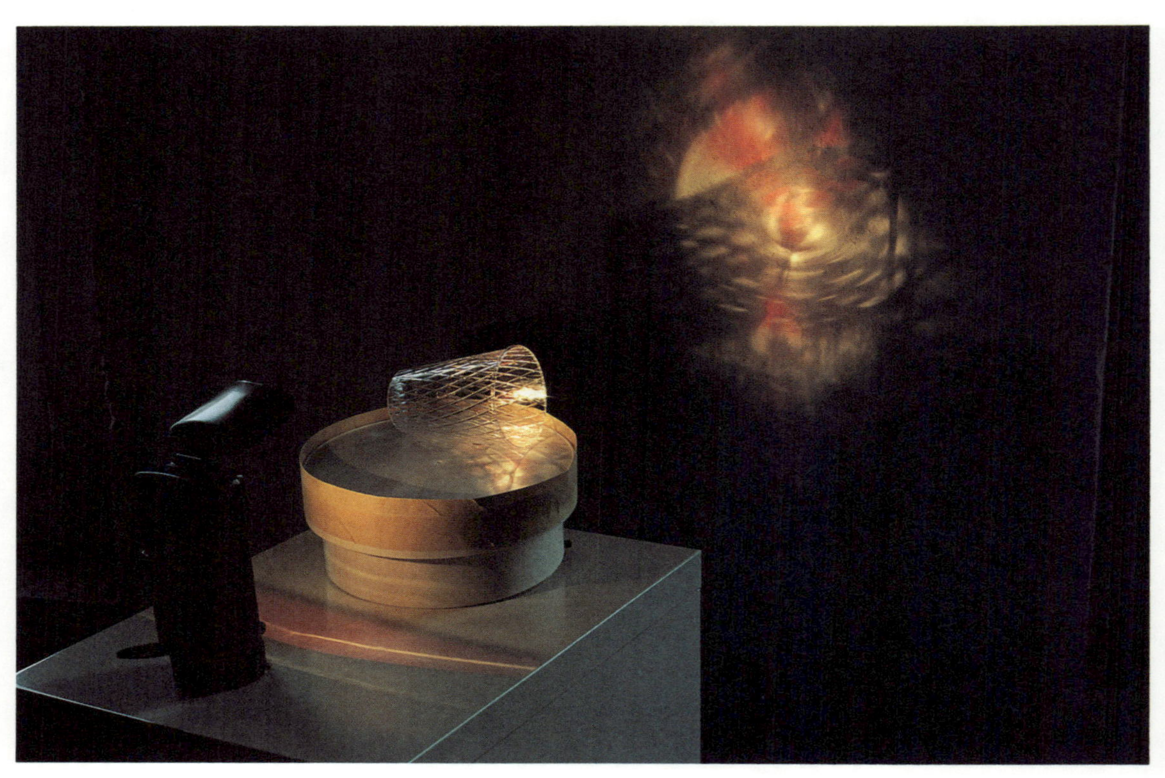

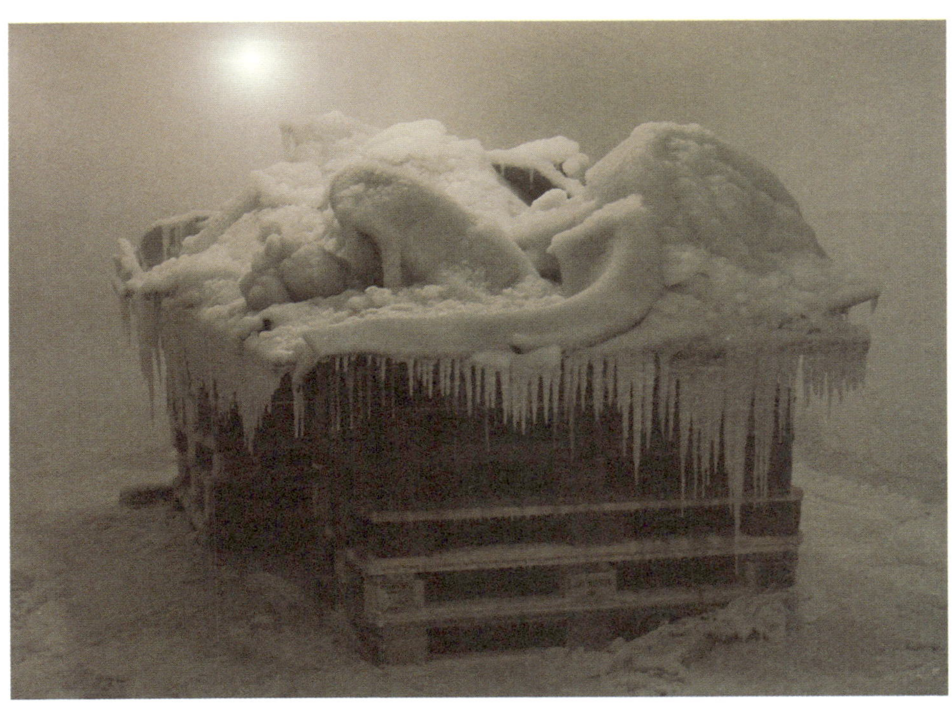

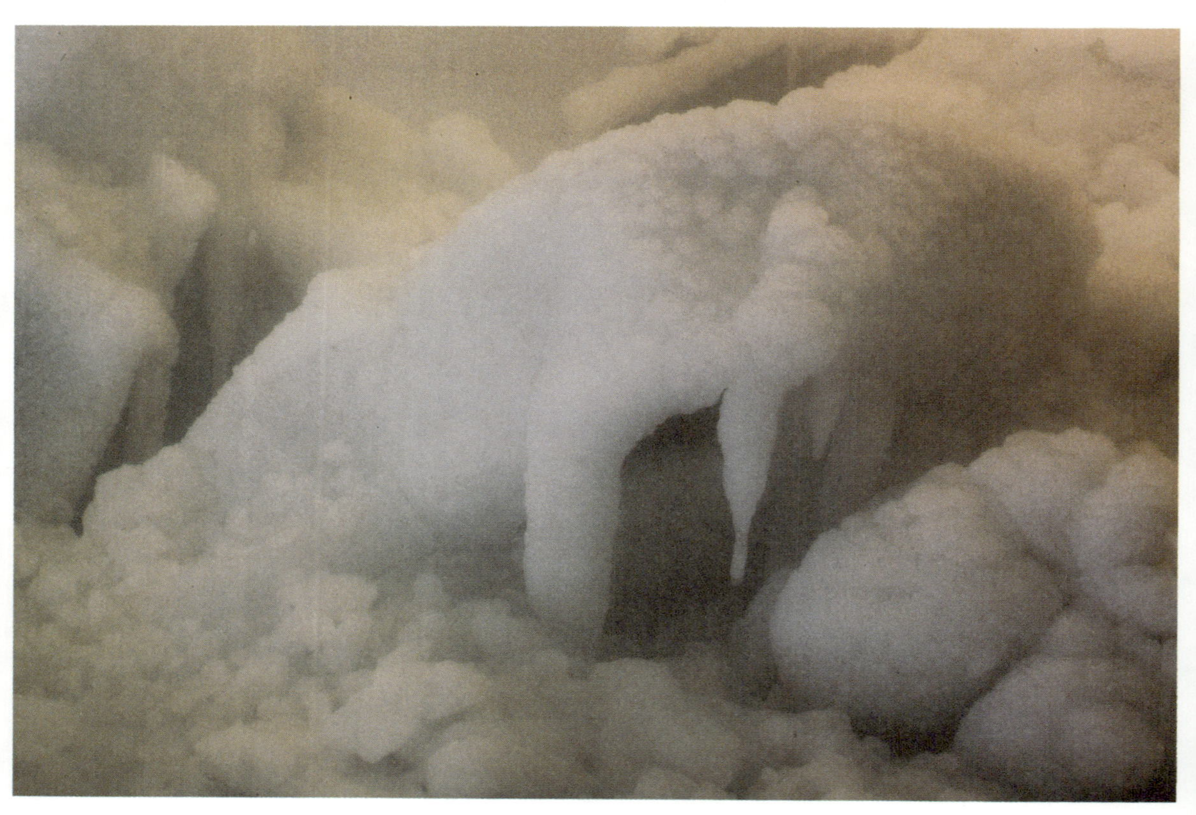

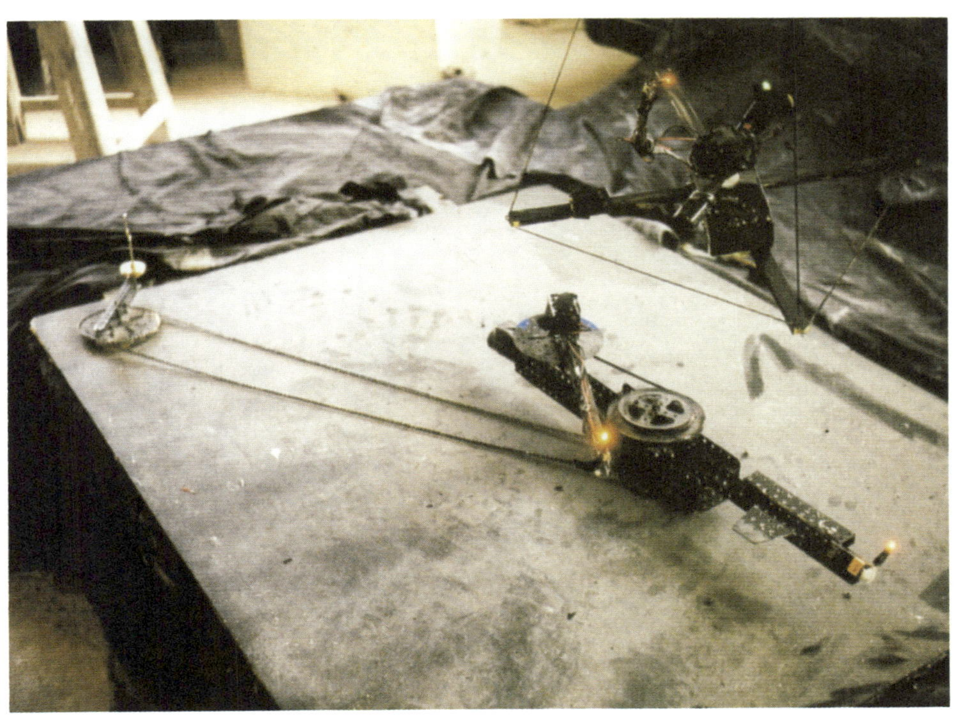

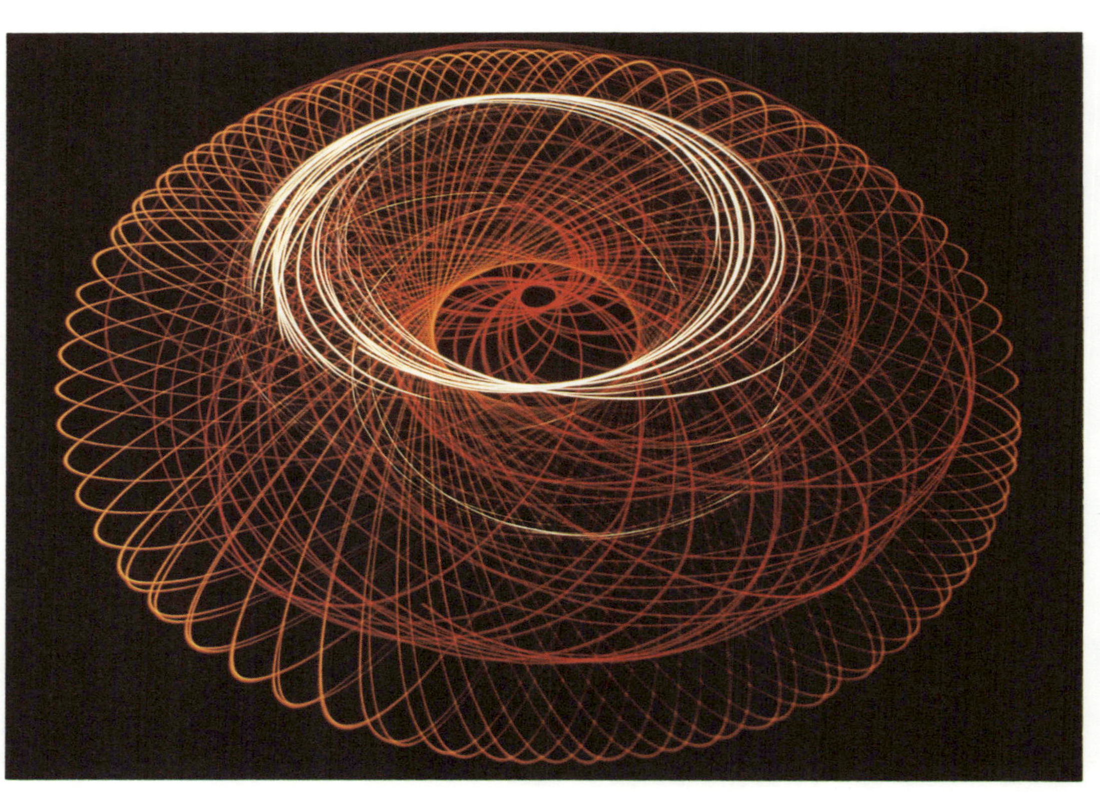

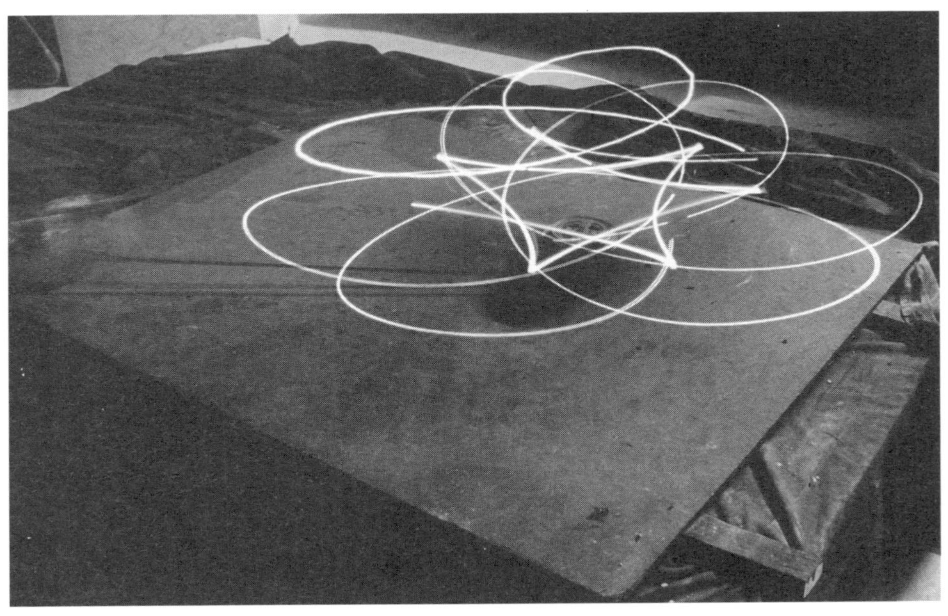

39   Surrlimachine in action

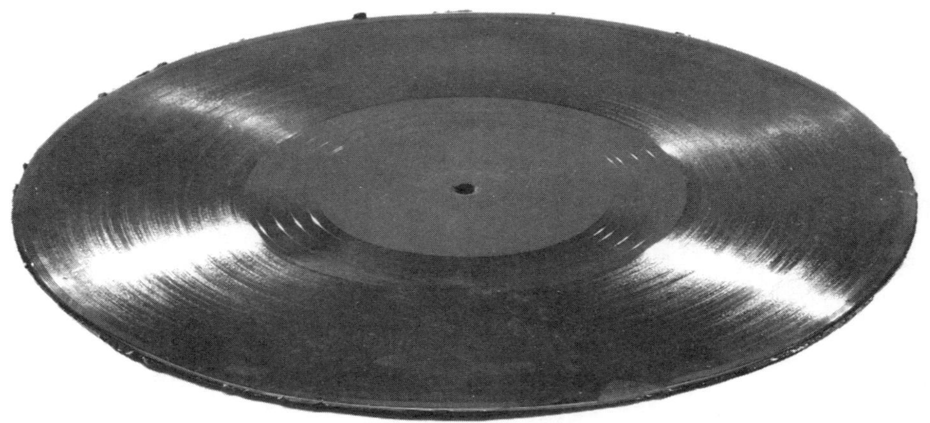

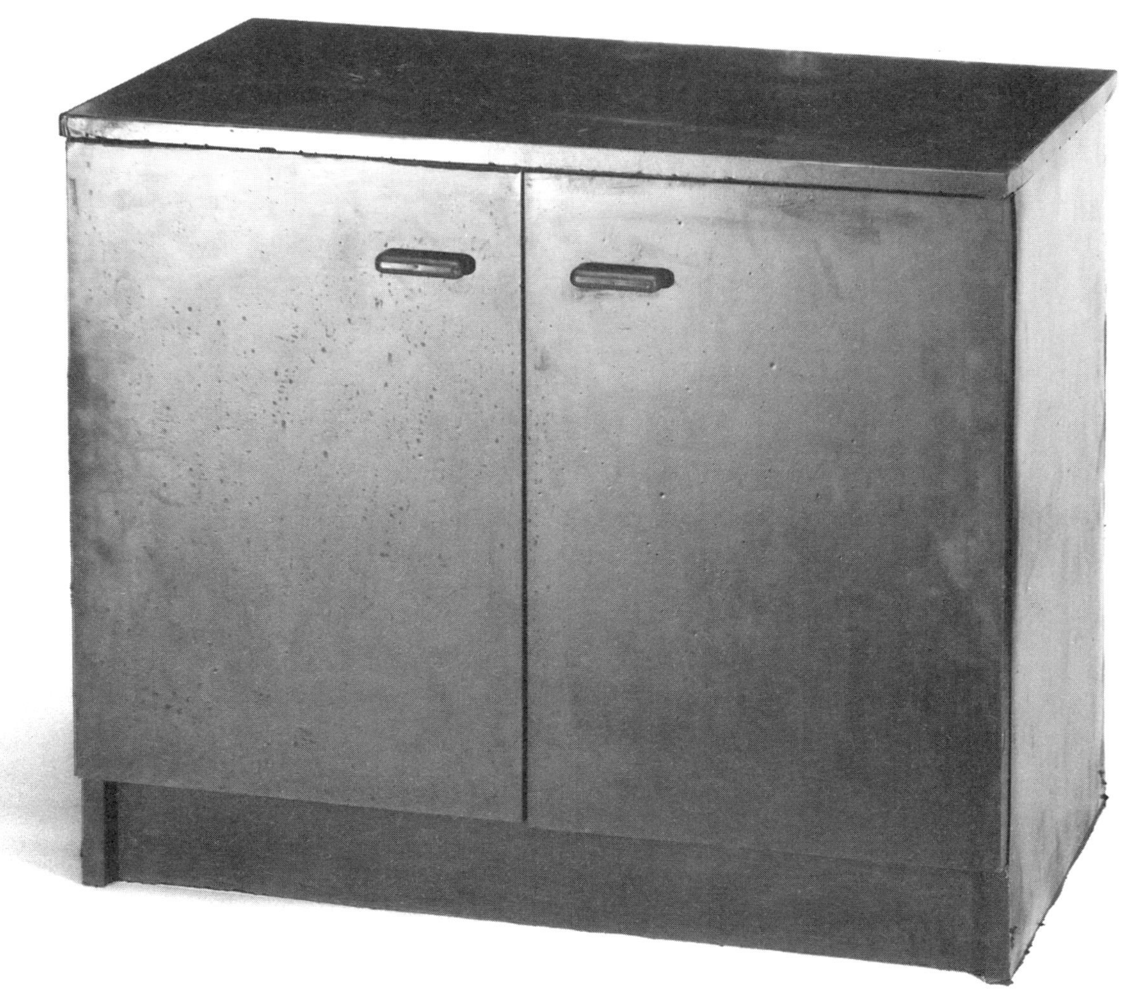

41 Cupboard

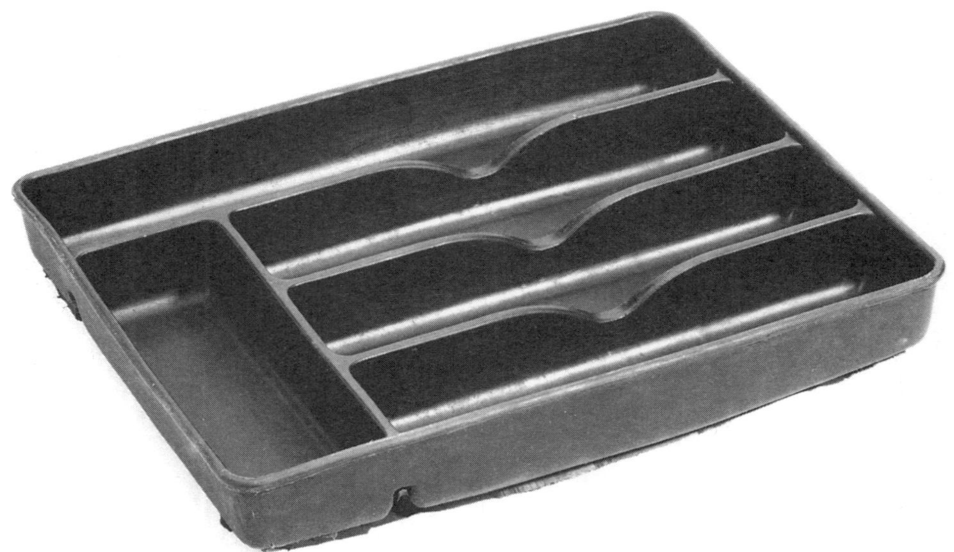

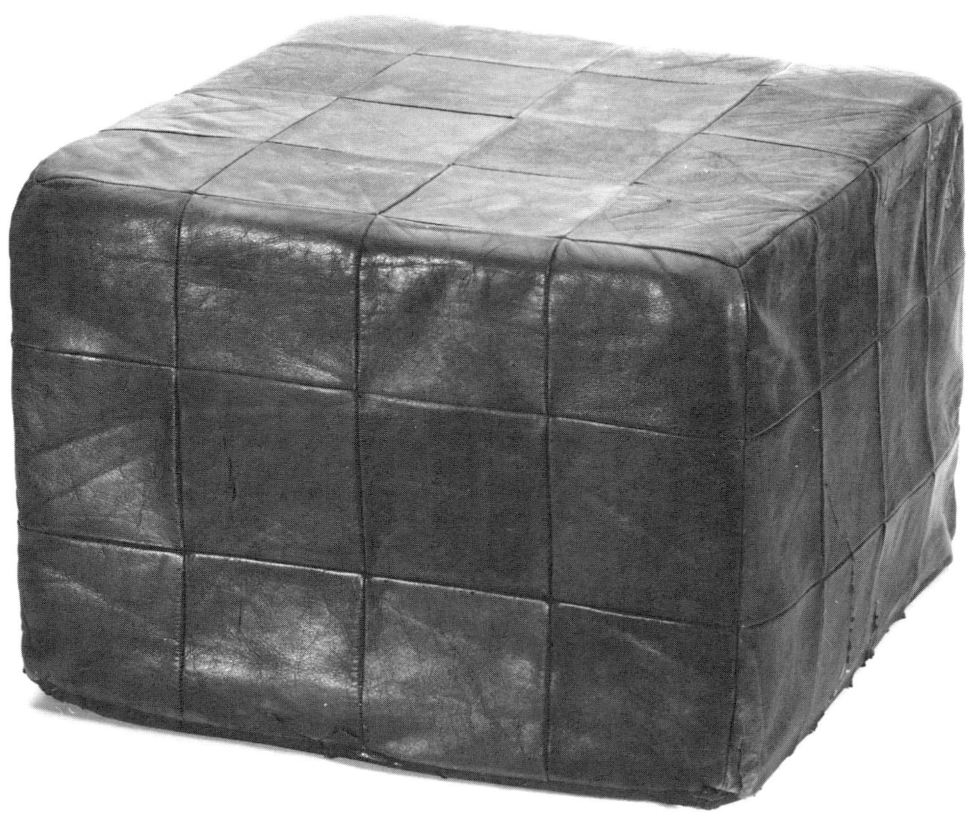

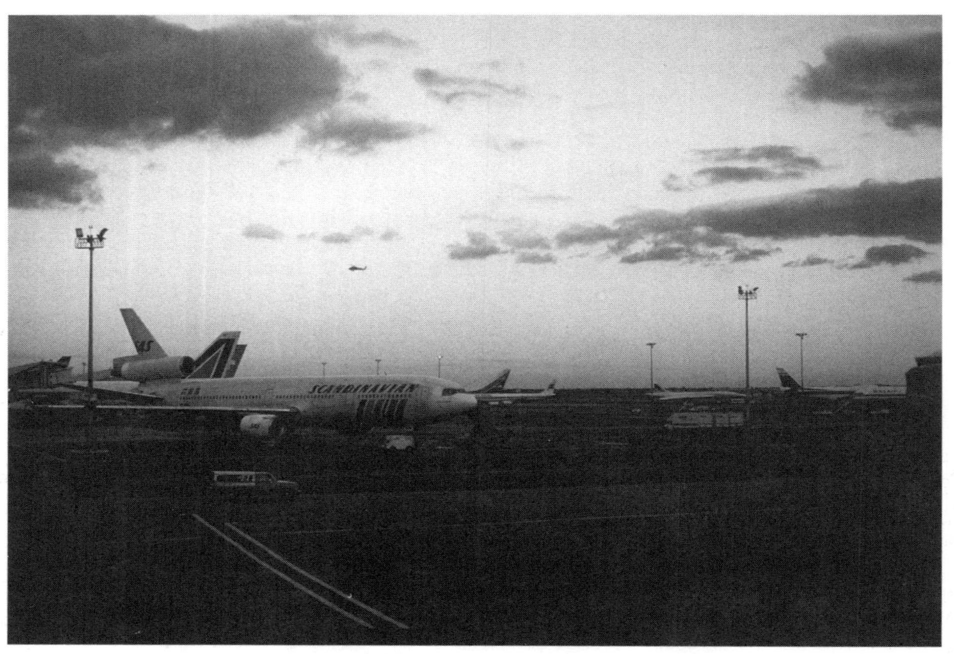

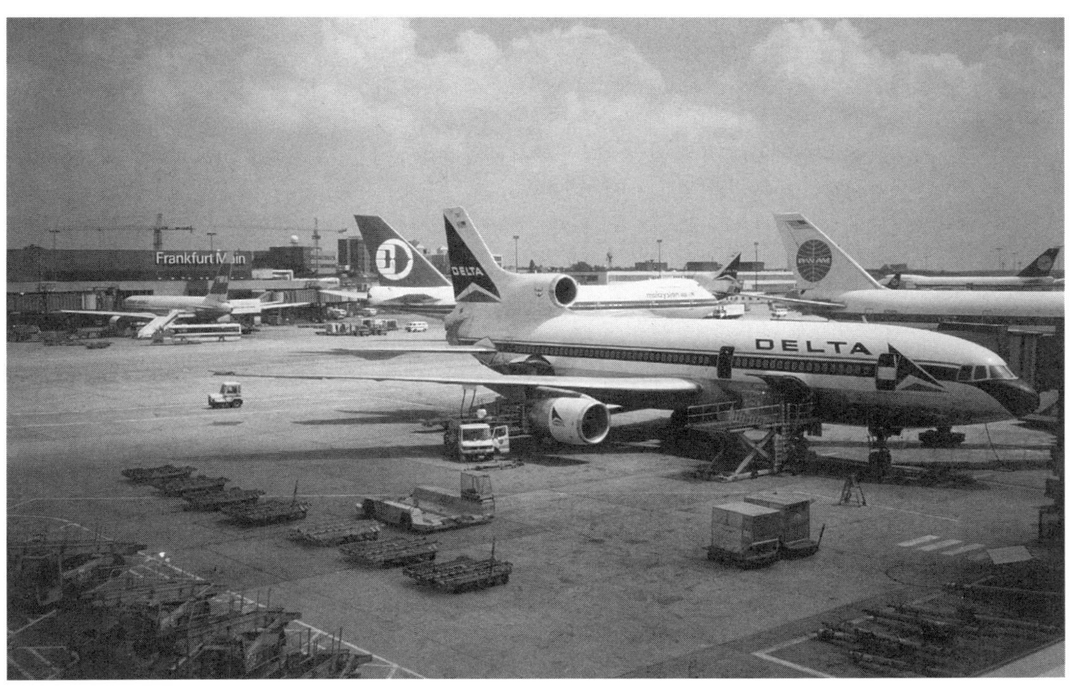

Frankfurt Main
DELTA
DELTA
PAN AM

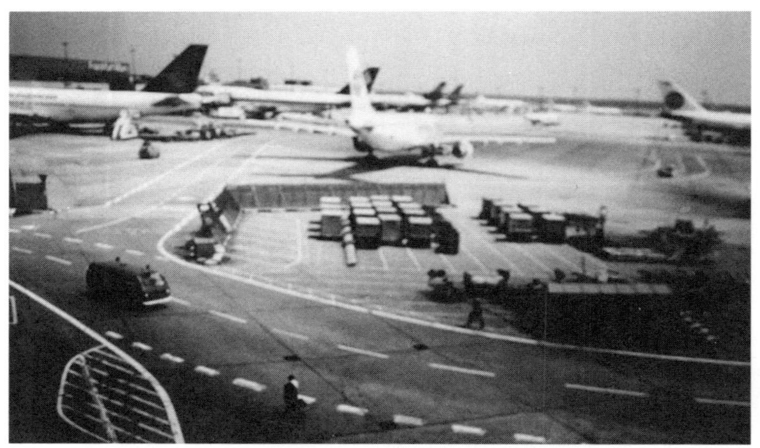

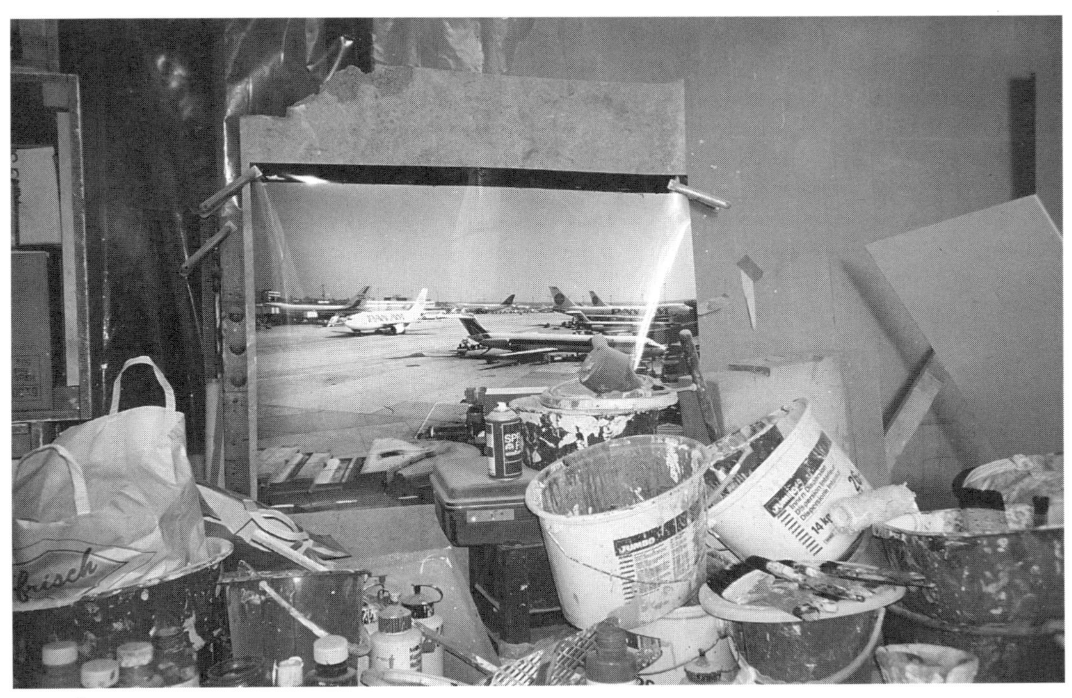

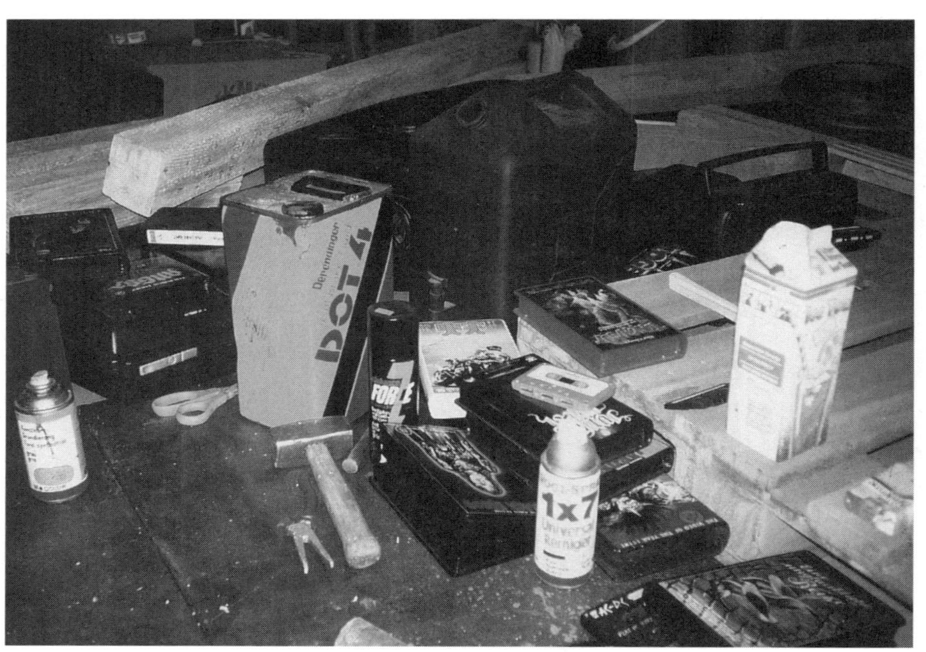

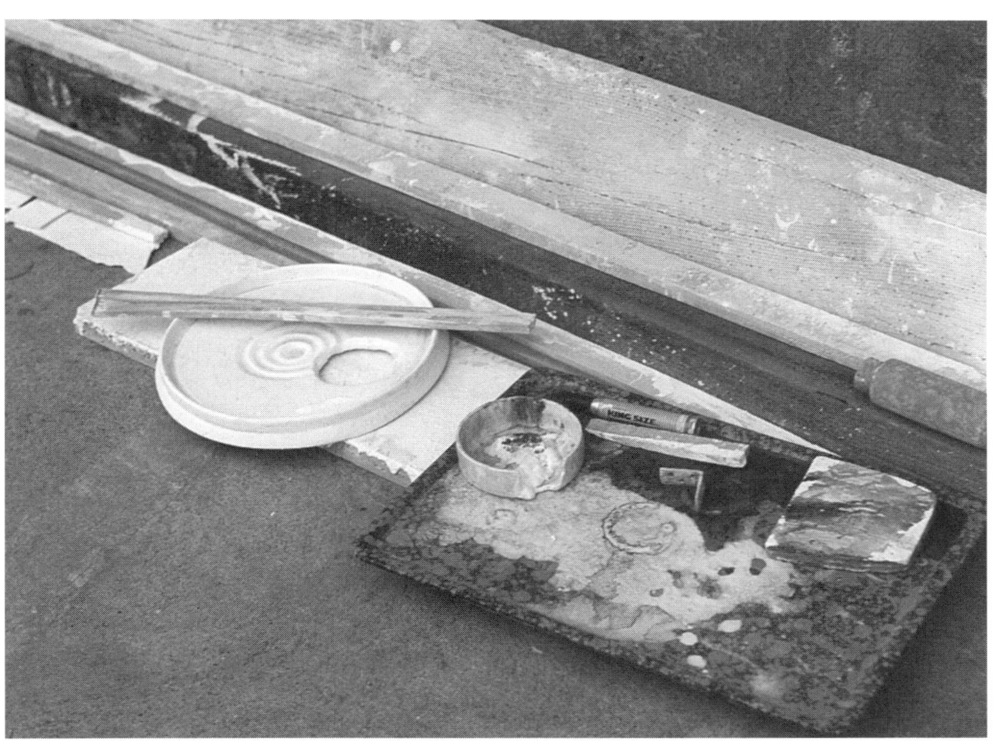

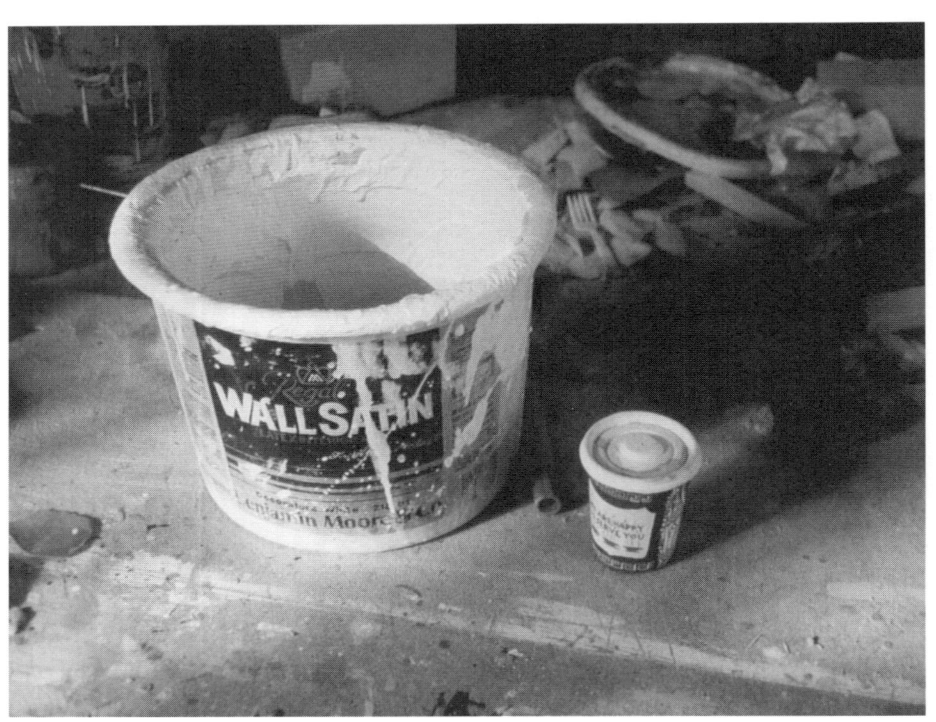
WALL SATIN
Benjamin Moore

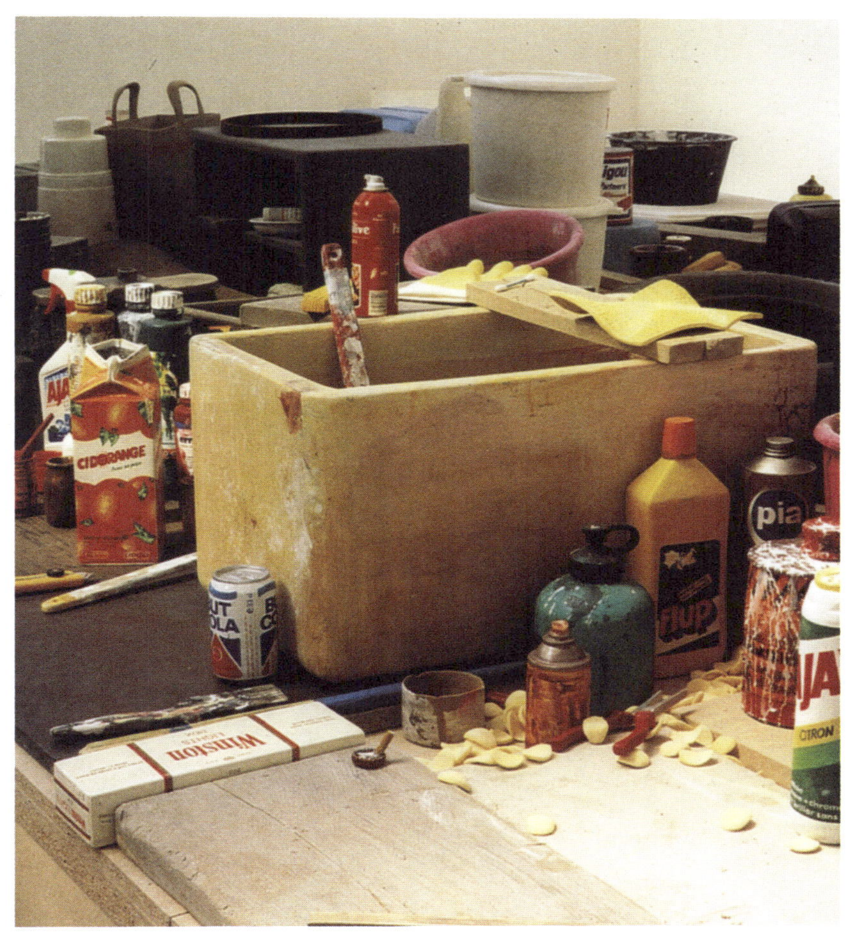

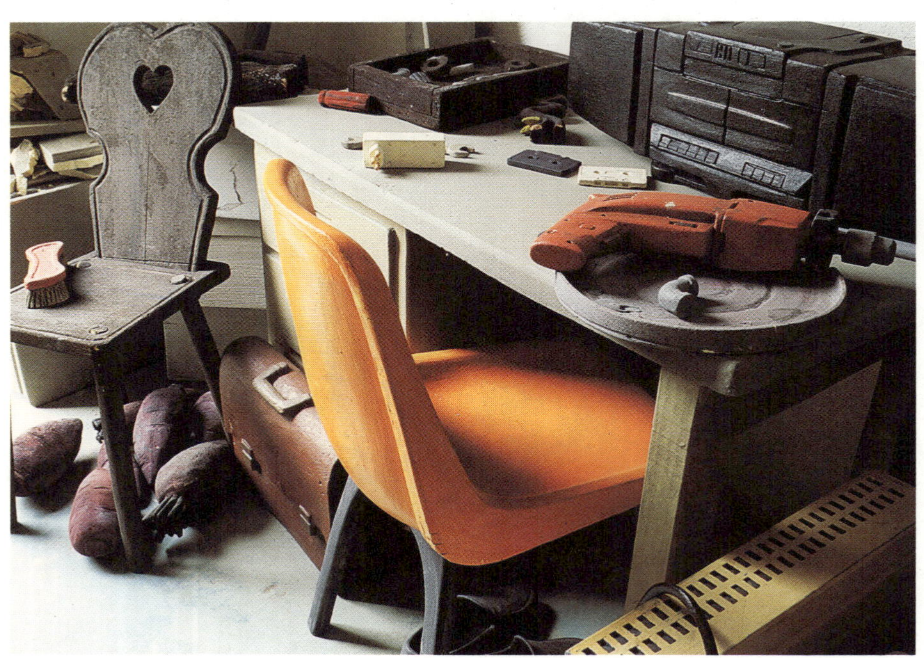

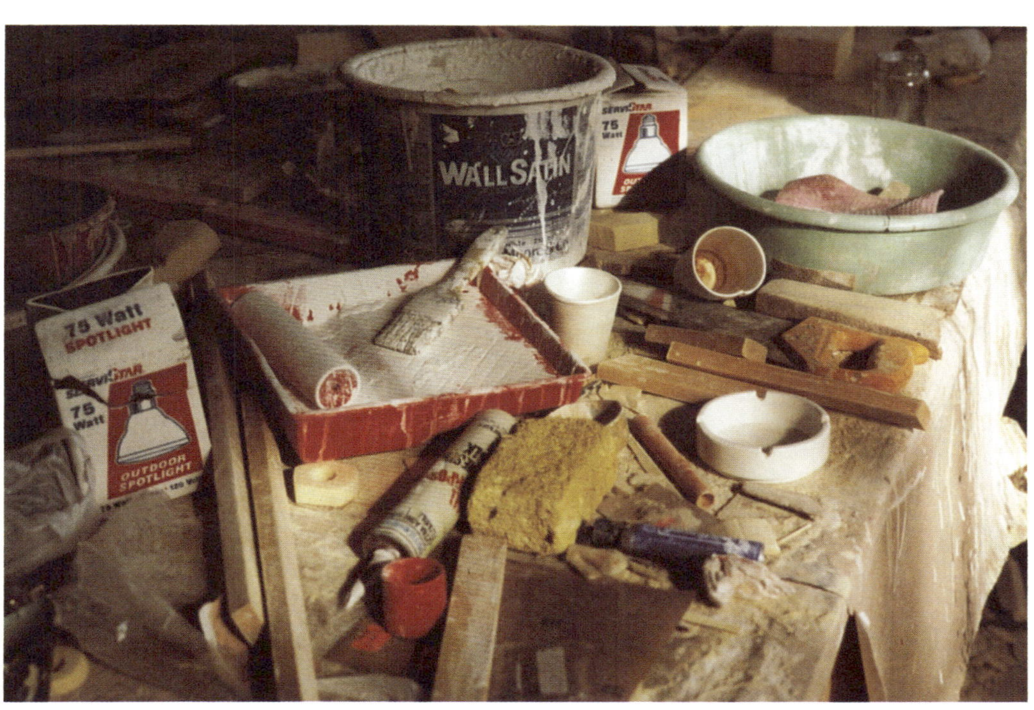

WALLSATIN
SERVISTAR
75 Watt
75 Watt
SPOTLIGHT
SERVISTAR
75 Watt
OUTDOOR
SPOTLIGHT

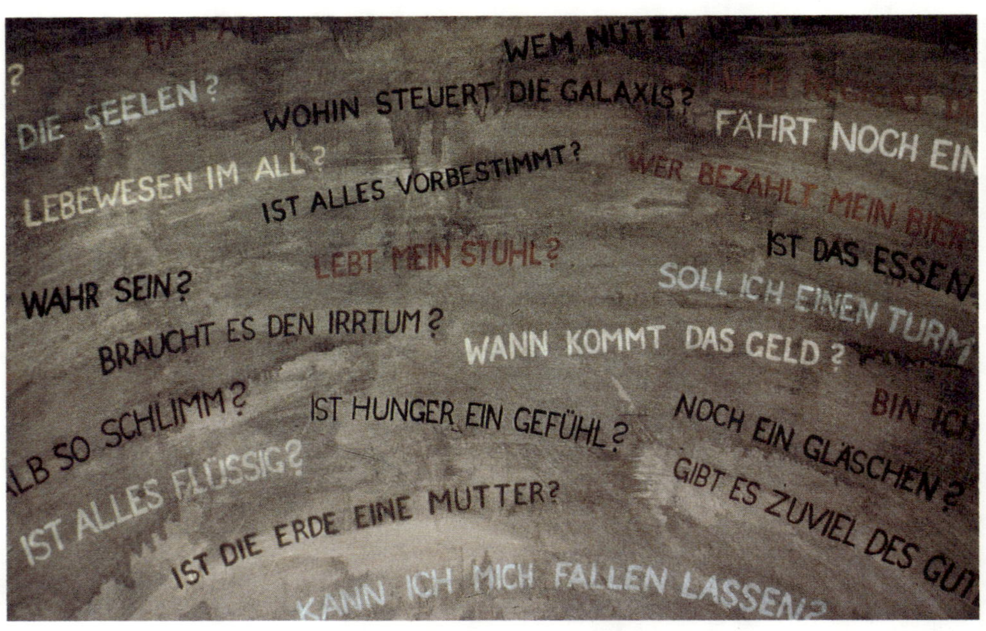
DIE SEELEN?
WOHIN STEUERT DIE GALAXIS?
WEM NÜTZT
FÄHRT NOCH EIN
LEBEWESEN IM ALL?
IST ALLES VORBESTIMMT?
WER BEZAHLT MEIN BIER
IST DAS ESSEN
LEBT MEIN STUHL?
SOLL ICH EINEN TURM
WAHR SEIN?
BRAUCHT ES DEN IRRTUM?
WANN KOMMT DAS GELD?
BIN ICH
LB SO SCHLIMM?
IST HUNGER EIN GEFÜHL?
NOCH EIN GLÄSCHEN?
IST ALLES FLÜSSIG?
GIBT ES ZUVIEL DES GUT
IST DIE ERDE EINE MUTTER?
KANN ICH MICH FALLEN LASSEN?

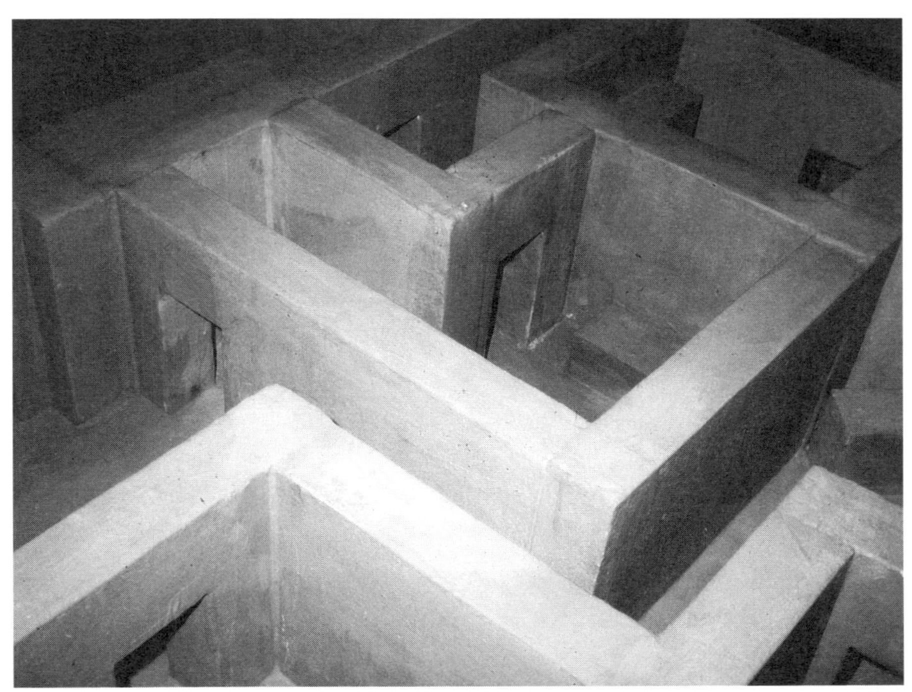

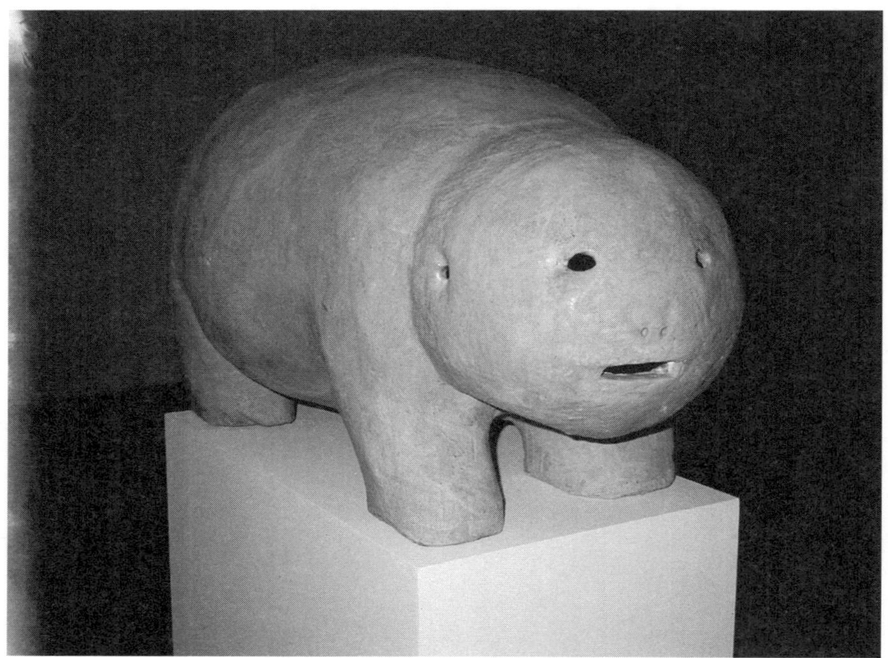

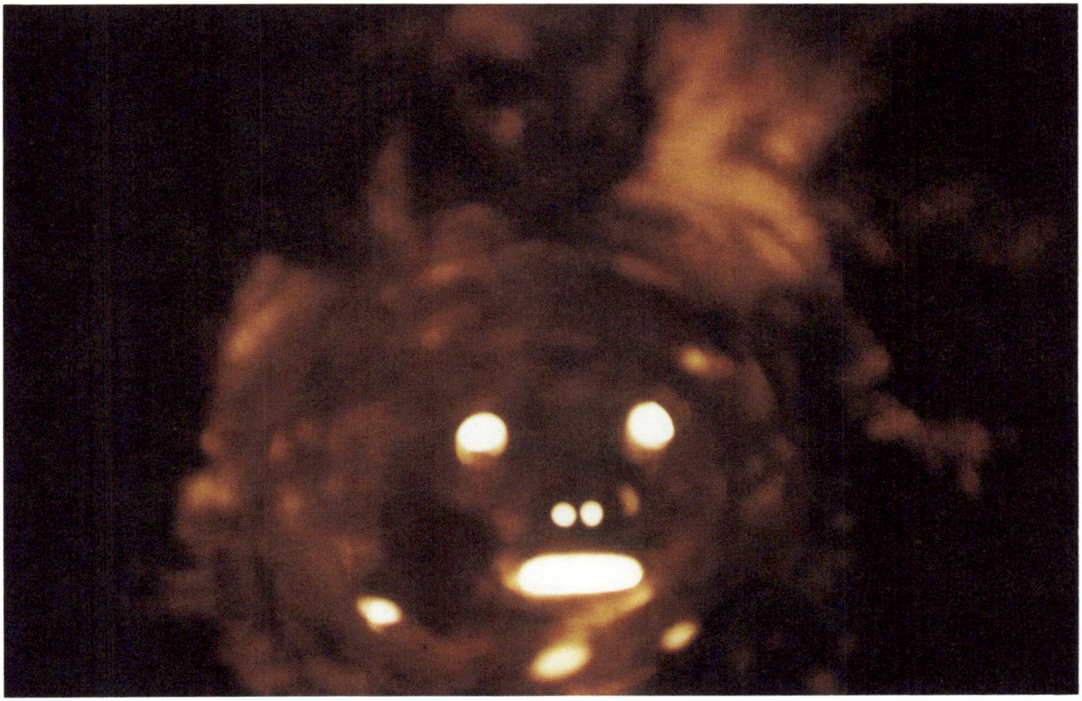

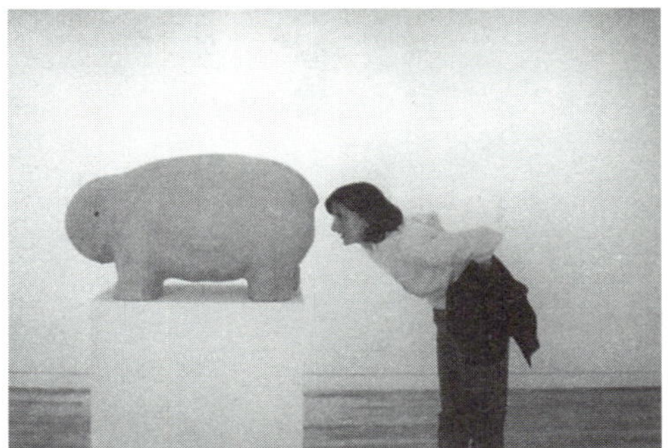

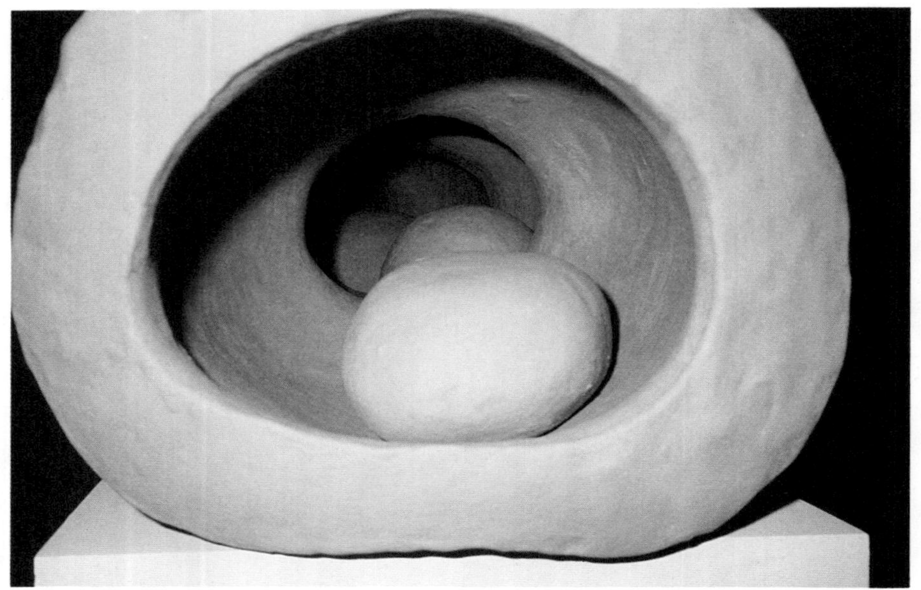

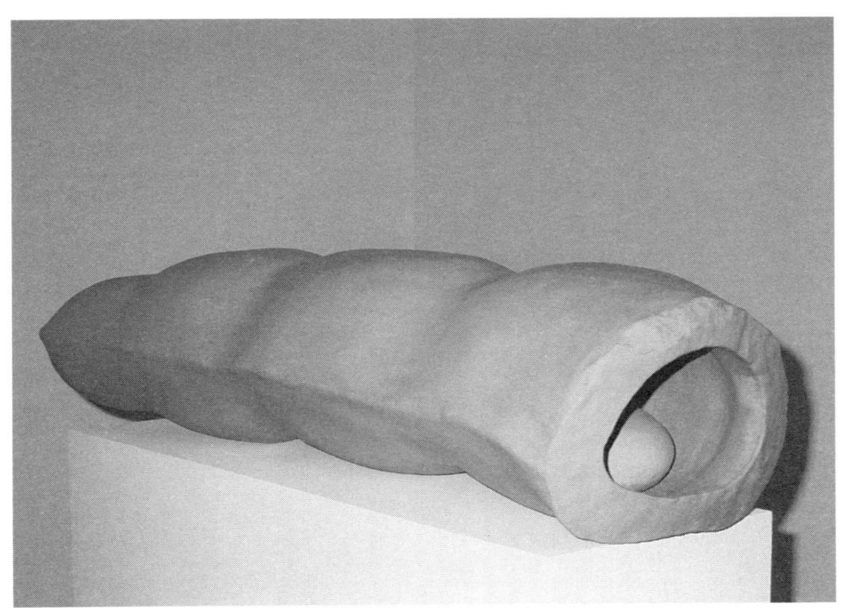

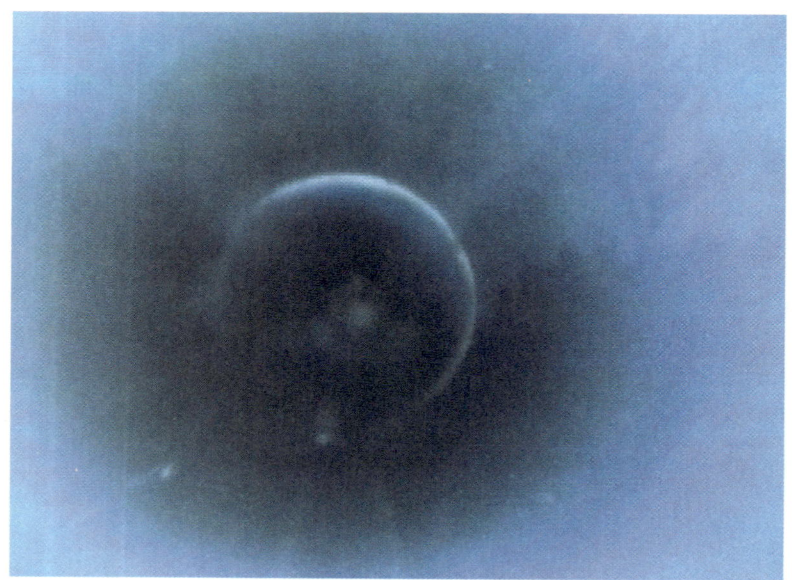

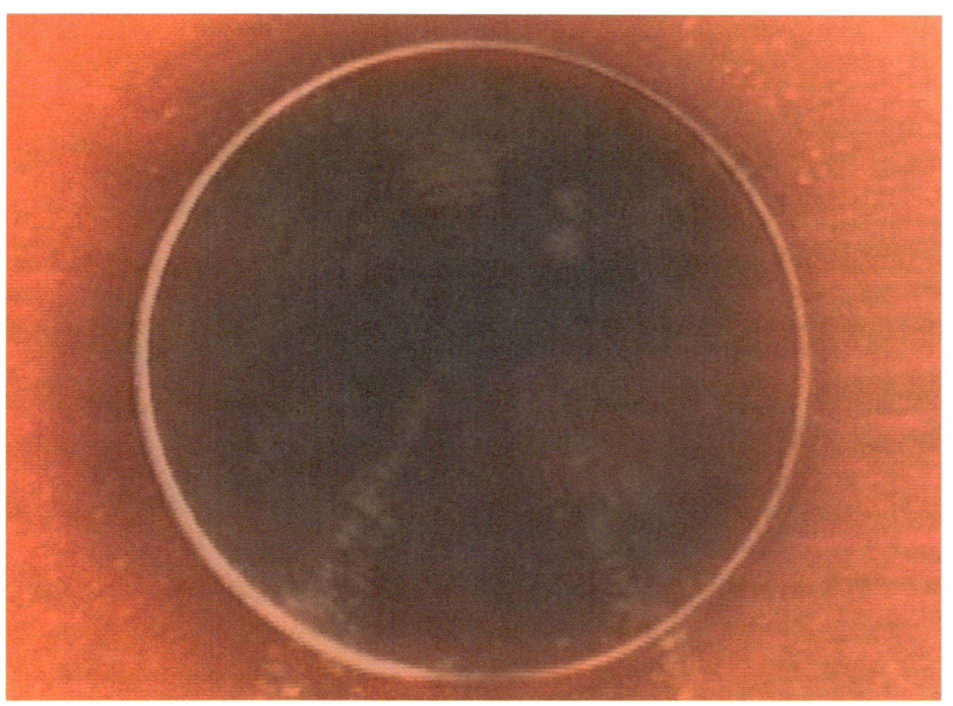

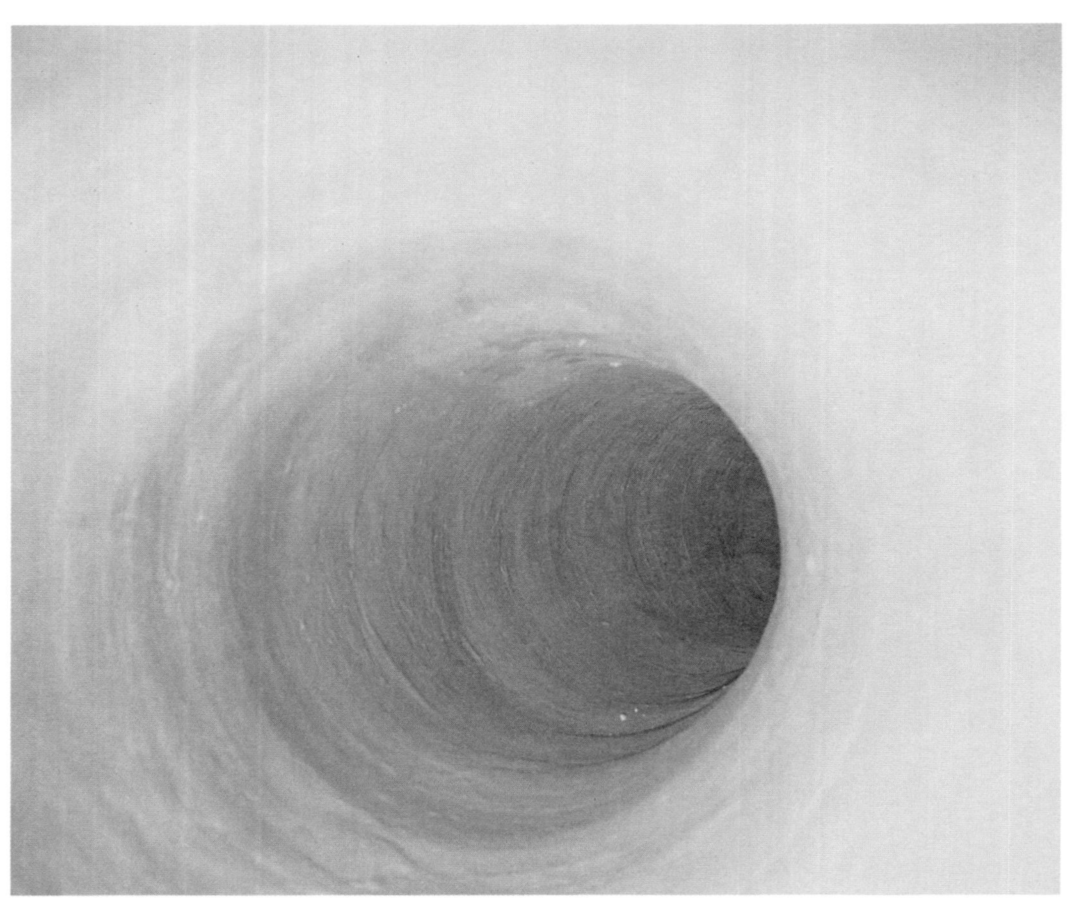

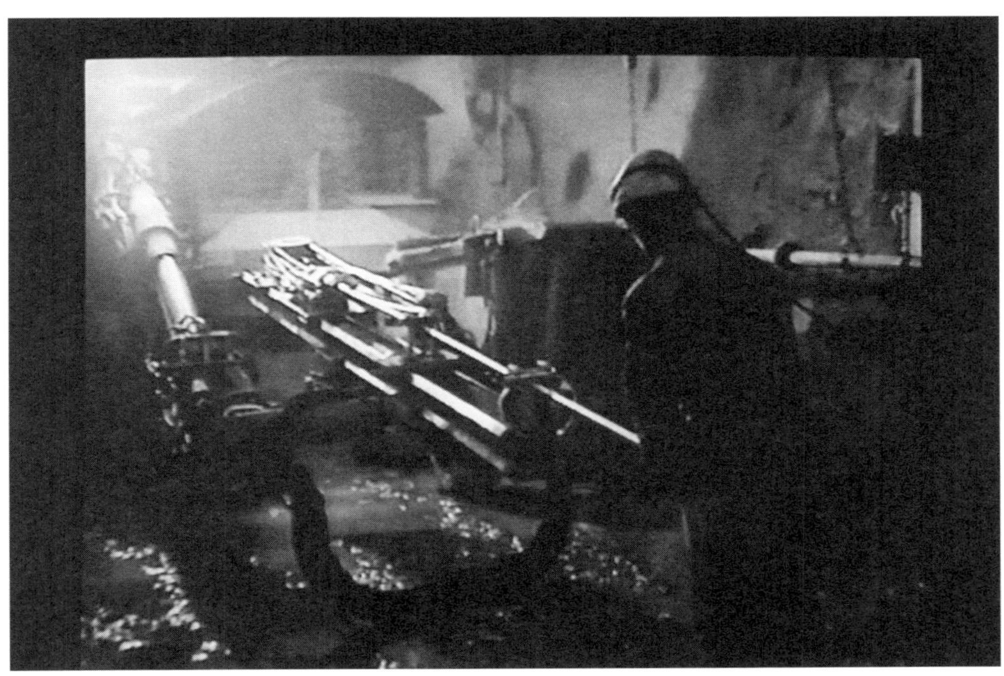

63   Construction workers in the Vereina Tunnel

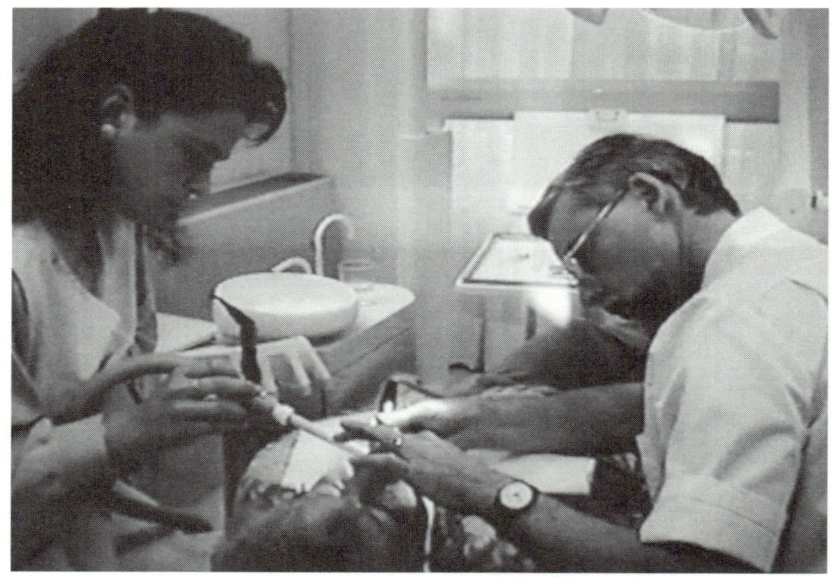

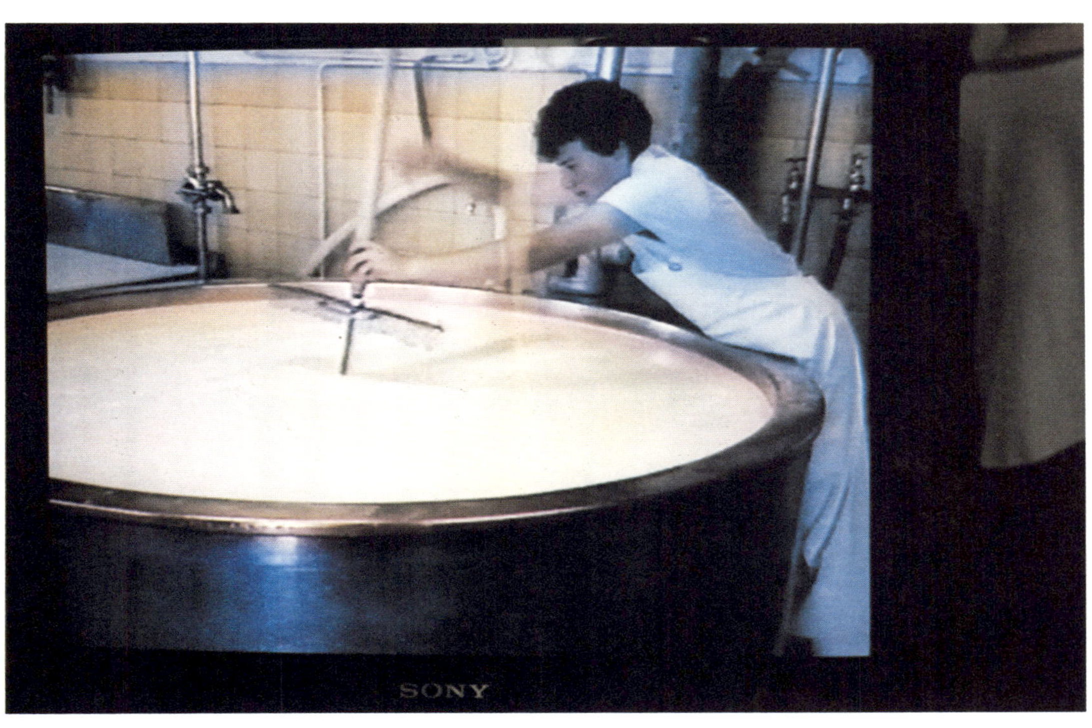

SONY

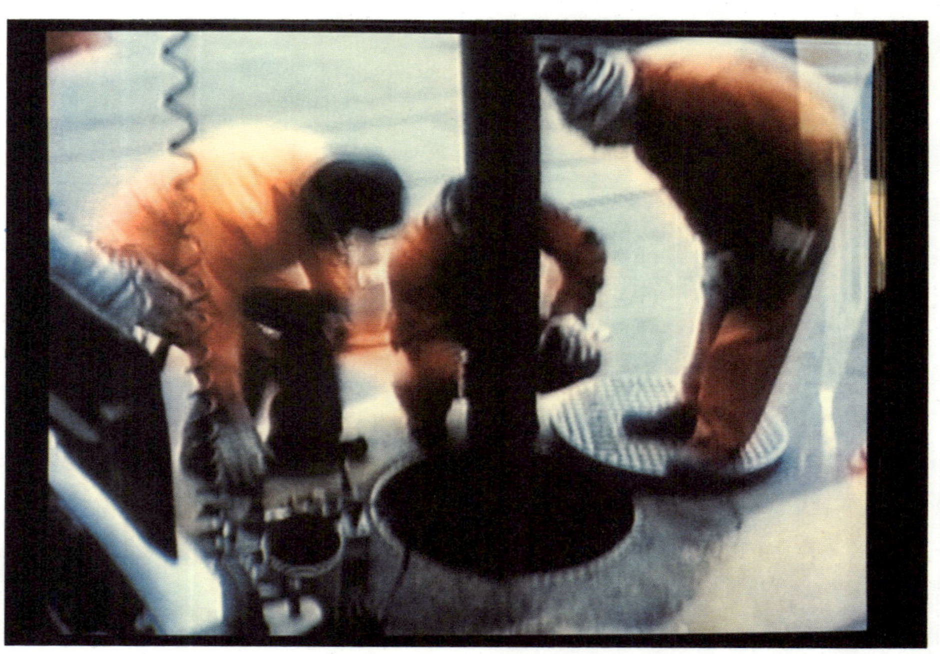

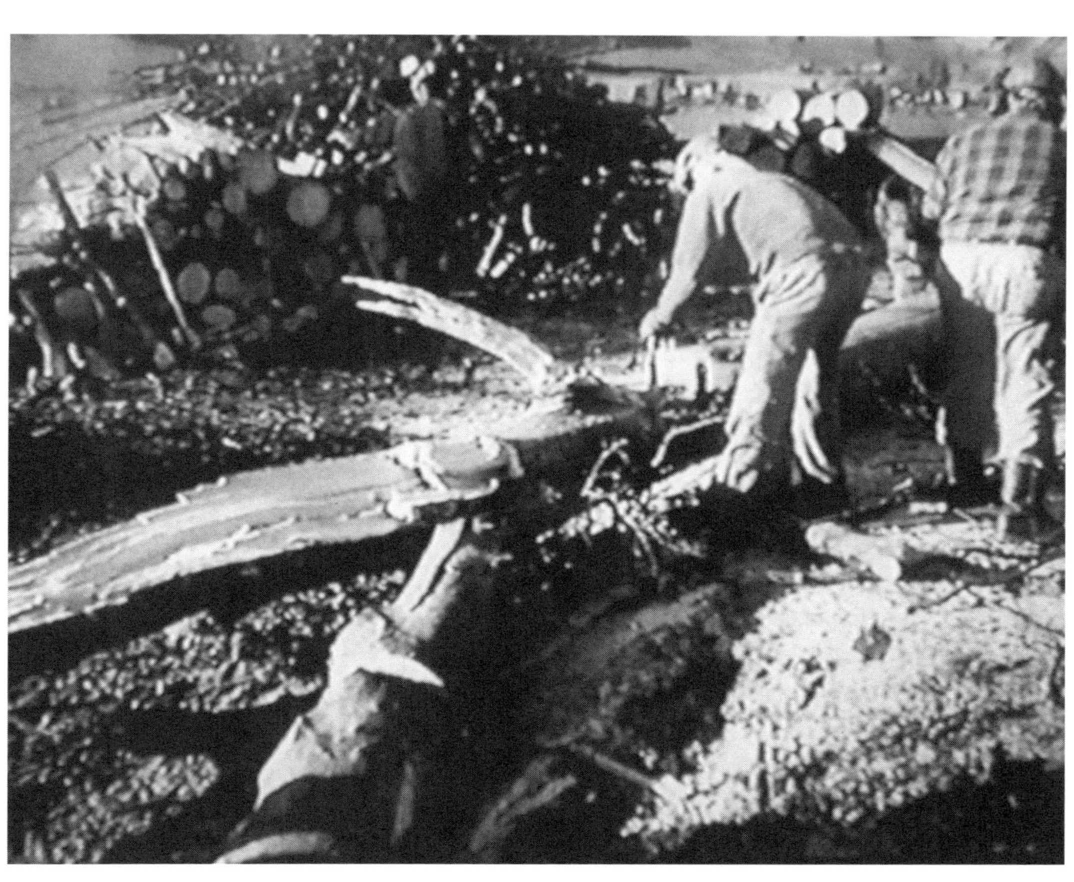

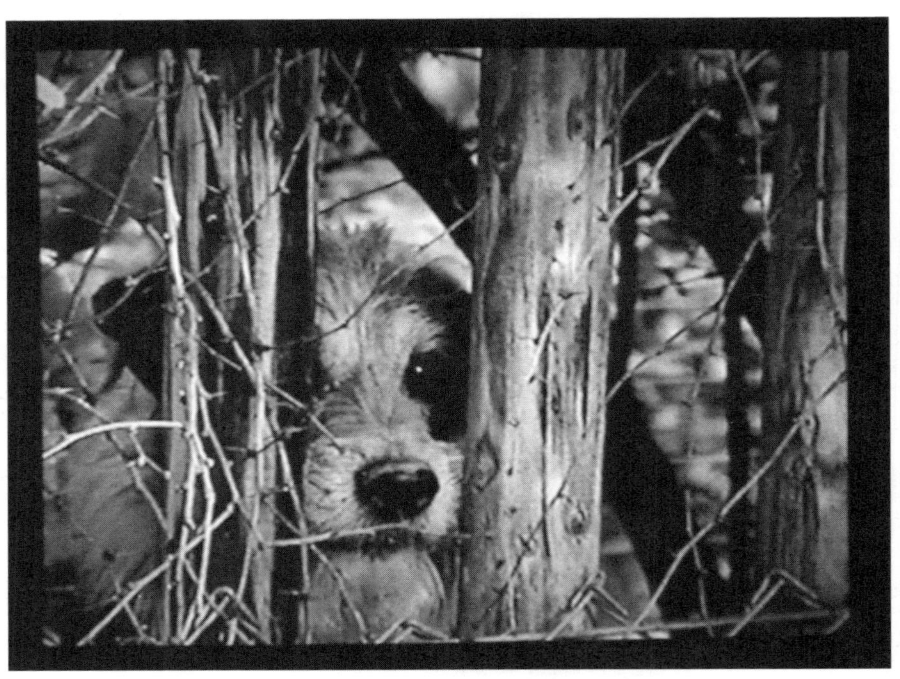

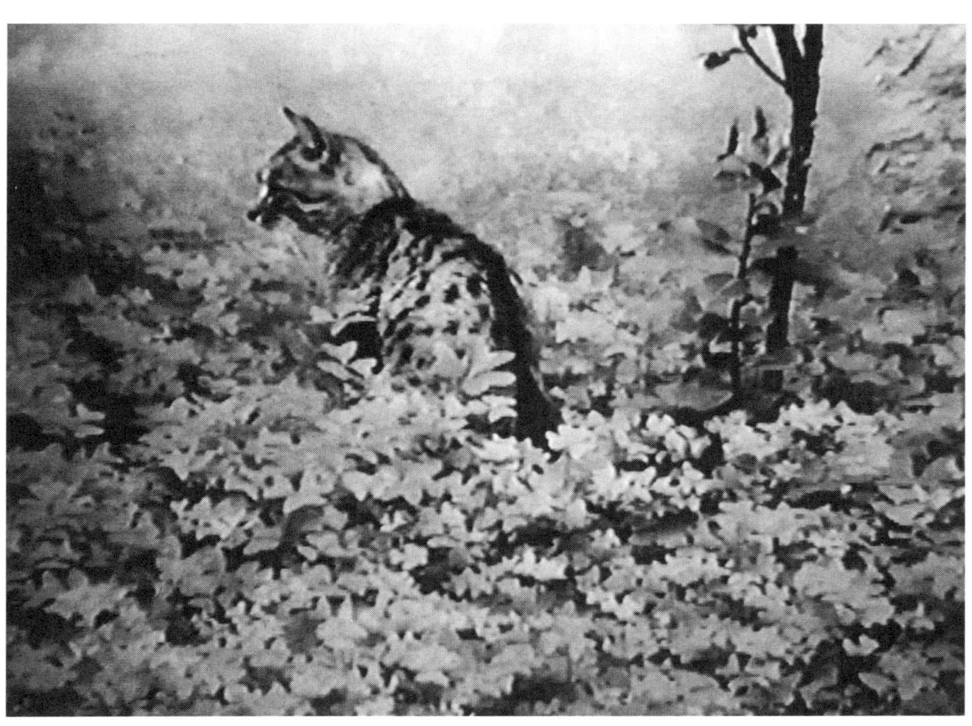

69   Cat in Venice

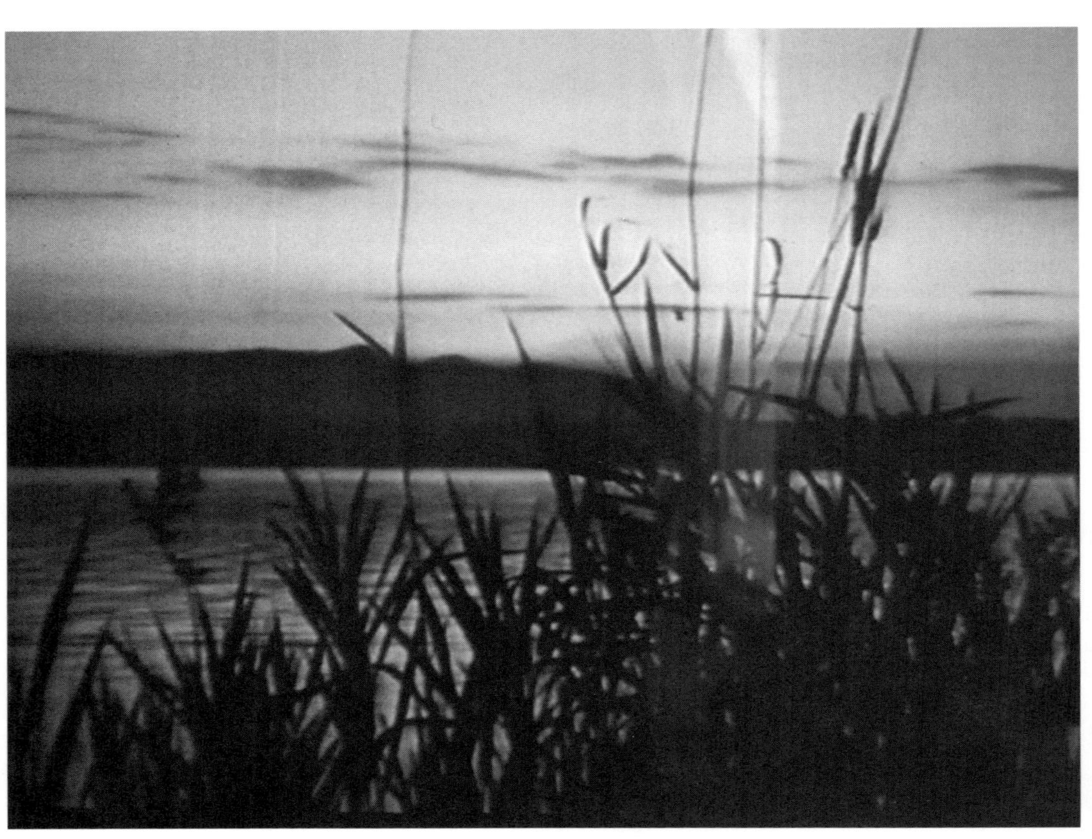

   Sunset at the Sihlsee

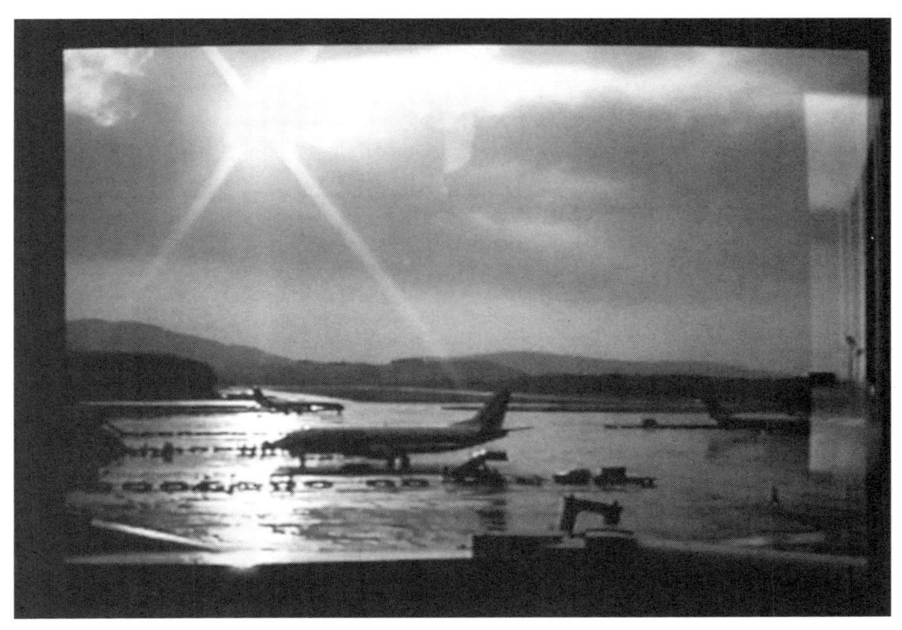

CAPTIONS (ALL WORKS ARE BY PETER FISCHLI AND DAVID WEISS)

1 *Dr. Hofmann on the first LSD trip*
from *Plötzlich diese Übersicht*
(Suddenly This Overview) 1981
unfired clay   Photo: Ywan Schumacher

2 *Anna O dreaming the first dream
interpreted by Freud*
from *Plötzlich diese Übersicht*
(Suddenly This Overview) 1981
unfired clay   Photo: Ywan Schumacher

3 *Hangout*
from *Plötzlich diese Übersicht*
(Suddenly This Overview) 1981
unfired clay   Photo: Ywan Schumacher

4 *Strangers in the night, exchanging glances*
from *Plötzlich diese Übersicht*
(Suddenly This Overview) 1981
unfired clay   Photo: Ywan Schumacher

5 *Peanuts*
from *Plötzlich diese Übersicht*
(Suddenly This Overview) 1981
unfired clay   Photo: Ywan Schumacher

6 *Street musician*
from *Plötzlich diese Übersicht*
(Suddenly This Overview) 1981
unfired clay   Photo: Ywan Schumacher

7 *In the cellar*
from *Plötzlich diese Übersicht*
(Suddenly This Overview) 1981
unfired clay   Photo: Ywan Schumacher

8–10 In the studio: unfinished sculptures
for the exhibition *Fieber (Fever)*
at Monika Sprüth Galerie, Cologne   1983
polyurethane

11 In the studio: *Idiot vert (Green Idiot)*
sculpture from the *Fieber (Fever)* series   1983
polyurethane, paint

12 *Mutterschwein mit Ferkeln (Pig and piglets)* 1983
polyurethane

13 *Slumberloop*
from *Stiller Nachmittag (Quiet Afternoon)*
1984–1985
black-and-white photograph

14 *Honour, Courage, Confidence*
from *Stiller Nachmittag (Quiet Afternoon)*
1984–1985
black-and-white photograph

15 *Outlaws*
from *Stiller Nachmittag (Quiet Afternoon)*
1984–1985
color photograph

16 *Quiet Afternoon*
from *Stiller Nachmittag (Quiet Afternoon)*
1984–1985
color photograph

17 *Dark Impulse*
from *Stiller Nachmittag (Quiet Afternoon)*
1984–1985
black-and-white photograph

18 *Mrs. Pear bringing her husband a freshly
ironed shirt for the opera. The boy smokes.*
from *Stiller Nachmittag (Quiet Afternoon)*
1984–1985
color photograph

19 *Hare*
from *Stiller Nachmittag (Quiet Afternoon)*
1984–1985
color photograph

20 *Lumpentiti (Cloth doll)*
from the installation at the Stock Market
Exchange, Zürich   1993
cloth and coins

21 *Schneemann (Snowman)*
New Year's card for the Energy Department,
Saarbrücken, Germany   1989

22 *In the Mountains*
from *Wurstserie*   1979
color photograph

23 *The Fire of Uster*
from *Wurstserie*   1979
color photograph

24 Building in Münster
part of the exhibition *Skulptur, Projekte,*
Münster, Germany   1987
wood, paint, Plexiglas

25–26 Details of #24

27 Cars in the studio   1988
plaster

28–31 Stills from *Der Lauf der Dinge
(The Way Things Go)*   1985–1987
16mm film   Camera: Pio Corradi

32 Vitrine with leftovers from *Der Lauf der Dinge
(The Way Things Go)*   1987

33 Leftovers from *Der Lauf der Dinge*
(*The Way Things Go*) 1987

34 *Son et lumière (Sound and Light)* 1990
flashlight, turntable, plastic cup, tape

35 Experiment for the project *Eislandschaft*
(*Ice-Landscape*)
for the Power Plant at Saarbrücken 1989
wood, metal, water

36 Detail of #35

37 Surrlimachine 1986
metal, wood, electric lamps, batteries, wire

38 *Surrli* 1986
Cibachrome

39 Surrlimachine in action 1986
metal, wood, electric lamps, batteries, wire

40 *Schallplatte (Record)* 1988
cast rubber, Beracryl
(playable cast of an unidentified soul record)

41 *Kästchen (Cupboard)* 1987
cast rubber, Beracryl

42 *Besteckbehälter (Divider)* 1987
cast rubber, Beracryl

43 *Hocker (Ottoman)* 1987
cast rubber, Beracryl

44–46 *Airports* 1988
Cibachrome

47 In the studio

48 In the studio: detail from *Der Tisch (The Table)*
1992
polyurethane, paint

49 Group of objects for Portikus, Frankfurt am Main
1993
polyurethane, paint

50 In the studio: preparation for the exhibition at
Sonnabend Gallery, New York 1994
polyurethane, paint

51 Detail from *Der Tisch (The Table)* at Kunsthalle
Zürich 1992–1993
polyurethane, paint

52 Room at the Hardturmstrasse 1990–1992
polyurethane, paint

53 In the studio: preparation for the exhibition at
Sonnabend Gallery, New York 1994
polyurethane, paint

54 Detail from *Fragentopf (Question Pot)* 1984
polyurethane, cloth, paint

55 Detail from *Apartment* 1984
polyurethane, cloth, paint

56 *Tier (Animal)* 1985
polyurethane, cloth, paint

57 Inside the animal 1985
polyurethane, cloth, paint

58 Inside the bean 1985
polyurethane, cloth, paint

59 *Bohne (Bean)* 1985
polyurethane, cloth, paint

60–61 *Kanalvideo (Canal Video)* 1992
video footage of Zürich sewage system canals
color videotape

62 *Röhre (Tube)* 1984
polyurethane, cloth, paint

63 Video still from the installation at the Swiss
Pavilion, Venice Biennale 1995
color videotape Photo: © Mancia/Bodmer

64 Video still from the installation at the Swiss
Pavilion, Venice Biennale 1995
color videotape Photo: © Mancia/Bodmer

65 Video still from the installation at the Swiss
Pavilion, Venice Biennale 1995
color videotape Photo: © Mancia/Bodmer

66 Video still from the installation at the Swiss
Pavilion, Venice Biennale 1995
color videotape Photo: © Mancia/Bodmer

67 Video still from the installation at the Swiss
Pavilion, Venice Biennale 1995
color videotape Photo: © Mancia/Bodmer

68 Video still from the installation at the Swiss
Pavilion, Venice Biennale 1995
color videotape Photo: © Mancia/Bodmer

69 Video still from the installation at the Swiss
Pavilion, Venice Biennale 1995
color videotape Photo: © Mancia/Bodmer

70 Video still from the installation at the Swiss
Pavilion, Venice Biennale 1995
color videotape

71 Video still from the installation at the Swiss
Pavilion, Venice Biennale 1995
color videotape

PETER FISCHLI
DAVID WEISS

IN A REST-LESS WORLD

WALKER ART CENTER

PETER FISCHLI AND DAVID WEISS: IN A RESTLESS WORLD

ORGANIZED BY ELIZABETH ARMSTRONG

WALKER ART CENTER MINNEAPOLIS
MAY 5 – AUGUST 11, 1996

INSTITUTE OF CONTEMPORARY ART, UNIVERSITY OF PENNSYLVANIA PHILADELPHIA
NOVEMBER 8, 1996 – JANUARY 17, 1997

WEXNER CENTER FOR THE ARTS, THE OHIO STATE UNIVERSITY COLUMBUS
FEBRUARY 8 – APRIL 13, 1997

SAN FRANCISCO MUSEUM OF MODERN ART
MAY 29 – AUGUST 31, 1997

THE INSTITUTE OF CONTEMPORARY ART BOSTON
OCTOBER 8, 1997 – JANUARY 4, 1998

KUNSTMUSEUM WOLFSBURG GERMANY
FEBRUARY 7 – MAY 3, 1998

A CONCURRENT EXHIBITION

PETER FISCHLI DAVID WEISS

ORGANIZED BY JONATHAN WATKINS
SERPENTINE GALLERY LONDON
JUNE 12 – JULY 21, 1996

UNLESS OTHERWISE NOTED, ALL WORKS ARE BY PETER FISCHLI AND DAVID WEISS.

COPYRIGHT AND LIBRARY OF CONGRESS CATALOGING-IN-PUBLICATION DATA
ARE FOUND ON PAGE 129 OF THIS BOOK.

FISCHLI WEISS IN

PAGES 1–71
ARTISTS' PAGES
PETER FISCHLI AND DAVID WEISS

PAGES 79–81
FOREWORD AND ACKNOWLEDGMENTS

PAGES 82–93
EVERYDAY SUBLIME
ELIZABETH ARMSTRONG

PAGES 94–113
PLAY/THINGS
ARTHUR C. DANTO

PAGES 114–121
THE SPEED OF ART
BORIS GROYS

PAGES 122–127
BIOGRAPHY
BIBLIOGRAPHY
EXHIBITION CHECKLIST
ROCHELLE STEINER

PUBLISHED BY **WALKER ART CENTER** MINNEAPOLIS
IN COLLABORATION WITH THE **SERPENTINE GALLERY** LONDON

GENEROUS SUPPORT FOR THE EXHIBITION
PETER FISCHLI AND DAVID WEISS: IN A RESTLESS WORLD
HAS BEEN PROVIDED BY PRO HELVETIA ARTS COUNCIL
OF SWITZERLAND, THE NATIONAL ENDOWMENT
FOR THE ARTS, LANNAN FOUNDATION, AND
SAMSUNG ELECTRONICS AMERICA, INC.

THIS BOOK WAS MADE POSSIBLE IN PART BY A GRANT FROM
THE ANDREW W. MELLON FOUNDATION
IN SUPPORT OF WALKER ART CENTER PUBLICATIONS.

MAJOR SUPPORT FOR WALKER ART CENTER PROGRAMS IS PROVIDED BY THE MINNESOTA
STATE ARTS BOARD THROUGH AN APPROPRIATION BY THE MINNESOTA STATE LEGISLATURE,
THE NATIONAL ENDOWMENT FOR THE ARTS, THE LILA WALLACE-READER'S DIGEST FUND,
THE BUSH FOUNDATION, THE McKNIGHT FOUNDATION, TARGET STORES, DAYTON'S, AND
MERVYN'S BY THE DAYTON HUDSON FOUNDATION, THE NORTHWEST AREA FOUNDATION,
THE GENERAL MILLS FOUNDATION, THE INSTITUTE OF MUSEUM SERVICES, BURNET REALTY,
THE AMERICAN EXPRESS MINNESOTA PHILANTHROPIC PROGRAM, THE HONEYWELL
FOUNDATION, NORTHWEST AIRLINES, INC., THE REGIS FOUNDATION, THE ST. PAUL
COMPANIES, INC., THE 3M FOUNDATION, AND THE MEMBERS OF THE WALKER ART CENTER.

THE SERPENTINE GALLERY GRATEFULLY ACKNOWLEDGES
FINANCIAL SUPPORT FROM THE ARTS COUNCIL OF ENGLAND
AND WESTMINSTER CITY COUNCIL.

MAJOR FUNDING FOR THE SERPENTINE GALLERY'S EXHIBITION PROGRAMME HAS BEEN RECEIVED
FROM ABSOLUT VODKA, A.F.A.A., PARIS AND THE FRENCH INSTITUTE, LONDON, BECK'S BIER,
BOELS & BÉGAULT, BORDEAUX WINES, HÄAGEN DAZS, MANGO RECORDS,
MEGELLAN INDUSTRIES PLC, PRUDENTIAL CORPORATION, REL CONSULTANCY GROUP,
SWISS ASSOCIATION OF PRIVATE COLLECTORS, TAG HEUER, AND VANITY FAIR.
TRUSTS AND FOUNDATIONS SUPPORTING THE EXHIBITION AND EDUCATION PROGRAMME
INCLUDE ARTHUR ANDERSEN & CO., THE BARING FOUNDATION, SIR JOHN CASS'S FOUNDATION,
THE JOHN S. COHEN FOUNDATION, THE ELEPHANT TRUST, J. PAUL GETTY JR. CHARITABLE TRUST,
THE HENRY MOORE FOUNDATION, THE NYDA AND OLIVER PRENN FOUNDATION, PRO HELVETIA,
VISITING ARTS, THE GOETHE-INSTITUT, THE STANLEY THOMAS JOHNSON FOUNDATION,
AND THE PO-SHING WOO CHARITABLE FOUNDATION.

Miracles interrupt the natural course of things, seeming to contradict the cosmic stories of which science is composed. A counterbalance to the rectitude of fact and the linearity of equations, miracles are the "big bang" result of faith. Despite the magnitude of such disequilibrium, the work of miracle makers often is disclosed through legible and empathetic acts that restore something crucial such as the loss of sight or physical momentum.

The Swiss artists Peter Fischli and David Weiss make secular miracles that return us to our senses. For fifteen years they have conspired collaboratively, blurring their respective identities and contributions as if to suggest that none of us are singular or sufficient. What we see first is something made together, something so seemingly simple that it may make us smile, an act of recognition that stresses the connection of one to another. We stop before and see the wonders often missed in our hurry to proceed through modern life. For a moment we regain something akin to the genetic structure of life, something essential yet small.

The intimacy and (misleading) simplicity of their work raises compelling questions about the relationship between making art and constructing a life of meaning. The studied innocence of their craft and imagery is a decoy, slowly luring the viewer below the placid surface of the familiar. While the purest definition of innocence is without gradation and devoid of evil, these two artists are self-conscious enough to recognize what any parent will report: the seeming innocence of a child's play often suggests disturbances that cannot safely or easily be brought to the surface. While the subjects of Fischli and Weiss's sculptures, photographs, installations, films, and videos could not be more transparent — a bowl of peanuts, a precariously balanced tower of functional objects, a janitor's closet — things are not what they first appear to be.

In realizing this publication — the first in English to provide a global view of Fischli and Weiss's extraordinary world — the Walker Art Center collaborated with the Serpentine Gallery, which will be presenting its own exhibition of the artists' work in London this summer. The pleasure of working together is most evident in our ability to publish a catalogue of ambition, which includes the visual compendium the artists designed for the front section of this book. We all are grateful for this opportunity to pause, reflect, and celebrate the miracles of everyday life.

KATHY HALBREICH   DIRECTOR   WALKER ART CENTER

JULIA PEYTON-JONES   DIRECTOR   SERPENTINE GALLERY

 ACKNOWLEDGMENTS

First and foremost, I would like to thank Peter Fischli and David Weiss. Their spirit of camaraderie and collaboration infuses both the exhibition design, which they will create for each venue on the tour, and this catalogue, for which they contributed a unique photographic resumé of their career. Their humor and inventiveness enlivened the entire exhibition process, and I am indebted to them for their spirited engagement in our project.

I also thank the two writers who joined me in preparing text for this catalogue. In addition to the artists' pages, we are honored to have had the contribution of Arthur C. Danto, whose essay sheds a philosophical light on the work and whose joy in the playfulness of Fischli and Weiss is highly contagious. We are also grateful to Boris Groys for permitting us to reprint his eloquent essay from the artists' catalogue for the 1995 Venice Biennale, which discusses their video work in both historical and contemporary contexts.

This publication and exhibition would not have been possible without the guidance and support of a number of individuals and institutions. We are grateful to PRO HELVETIA Arts Council of Switzerland for their critical funding of this project. We were also fortunate to receive important grants from the National Endowment for the Arts and Lannan Foundation. Samsung Electronics America, Inc. made a crucial in-kind donation in support of the exhibition; special thanks are due here as well to Robert Bossman for his efforts on our behalf. This book was made possible in part by support from the Andrew W. Mellon Foundation and in collaboration with the Serpentine Gallery, where I had the good fortune to work with colleagues Jonathan Watkins and Julia Peyton-Jones.

We are always appreciative of those lenders who are willing to part with key works from their collection for a touring exhibition. In this regard, we are especially thankful to Anna Grässlin for her generosity. We also thank Andreas Meier at Centre Pasqu Art, Biel, Switzerland; Christian Klemm at Kunsthaus Zürich; Monika Sprüth at Monika Sprüth Galerie, Cologne; and Ileana Sonnabend and Antonio Homen at Sonnabend Gallery, New York, for their help with loans. Special thanks to Urs Staub, Swiss Commissioner for the 1995 Venice Biennale, and the Bundesamt für Kultur, Bern.

The participation of the other arts institutions on the exhibition tour has extended the life of our project, and we are pleased to acknowledge and thank key participants at the following museums: Patrick Murphy, Institute of Contemporary Art, Philadelphia; John R. Lane and

Gary Garrels, San Francisco Museum of Modern Art; Sherri Gelden, Sarah Rogers, and William Horrigan, Wexner Center for the Arts, Columbus, Ohio; Milena Kalinovska and Christoph Grunenberg, The Institute of Contemporary Art, Boston; and Gijs van Tuyl and Veit Görner, Kunstmuseum Wolfsburg, Germany.

Finally, I thank my many colleagues at the Walker Art Center for contributing their passion and expertise to this project. Walker Director Kathy Halbreich has been enormously supportive of the exhibition from the start, as has Gary Garrels, former Senior Curator. His successor, Chief Curator Richard Flood, arrived with great enthusiasm for the artists and for the project, and he has generously offered his advice and insights along the way. Bruce Jenkins, Film/Video Curator, has also given much time and thought to the exhibition and related programs. Walker Registrar Gwen Bitz has worked her usual magic to bring together the myriad works in the exhibition in a timely and safe manner. Kirk McCall and Peter Murphy of the Walker's exhibition crew likewise have brought their combined professionalism to bear on the exhibition's design and installation. Senior Graphic Designer Matt Eller worked closely with the artists to create a catalogue that is exceptionally well-tuned to the sensibility of his subject. Also in our Design Department, I thank Michelle Piranio for wearing many hats and always well; Kathleen McLean, for her able editorial advice; and Jeff Cashdollar, for the investment of many production hours in this project. Special thanks go to Janet Jenkins for working with me again and for her editorial rigor. Thanks also to our Development Department for their heroic efforts on behalf of the exhibition, and especially to Aaron Mack and Sarah Schultz for their energy and perseverance. I am indebted as well to Howard Oransky, Assistant to the Director for Program Planning, whose organizational clarity helped smooth the road for the exhibition's tour. Among the many others here whose participation has been greatly valued, I thank Therese Buchmiller, Michelle Coffey, Jacqueline Copeland, Katharine DeShaw, Siri Engberg, Karen Gysin, Irene Hoffman, Pam Jones, John Killacky, Karen Moss, Ariel Muller, Mary Polta, Jon Voils, and Cameron Zebrun. Thanks also to Meg Gravelle and the guard staff for going above and beyond their usual call of duty in the galleries. Along these lines, I am grateful to Rhonda Loverude, Assistant to the Curators, for her attention to the many details surrounding this exhibition. Last but not least, I am greatly appreciative of the unflagging efforts and support of Rochelle Steiner, National Endowment for the Arts Intern, for her commitment to this project and her exceptional contributions to virtually every aspect of the exhibition and catalogue.

ELIZABETH ARMSTRONG CURATOR

EVERYDAY SUBLIME

One of the most enduring and endearing aspects of the work of Swiss artists Peter Fischli and David Weiss is their fondness for everyday things. It is present in their first collaborative art project, *Wurstserie*, 1979, in which various types of meats and sausages animate scenes with such subversively generic titles as *In the Mountains* (figure 1) and *In the Carpet Shop* (page 101). It is still evident in their recent polyurethane sculptures of studio paraphernalia and in their ninety-six-hour videotape installation unreeling scenes of everyday life in Switzerland, shown at the Venice Biennale in 1995.

The *Wurstserie* not only introduced a vocabulary of homely objects that would be refined and redefined by the artists in the years to come, but also suggests a variety of other persistent themes and conundrums that inform their work across genres and time. The economy of means used to create these images, which are composed almost entirely from kitchen and household goods, still forms a pivotal locus in Fischli and Weiss's aesthetic. Likewise, the playful sensibility of the artists, albeit with its undercurrent of agitation, continues to attract notice. (Arthur Danto's essay in this volume addresses this aspect of the artists' work in great depth.) Indeed, the almost childlike spirit of discovery exhibited in the artists' work from its beginnings has persisted across the range of their various artistic endeavors — photographs, sculptures, videos, films, installations — and there continues to be something quite disarming about it. Finally, there are questions raised in this first project about the motivation of these two artists, about the nature of their collaboration, and about the meaning of their work that bear investigation throughout the artists' careers.

Plötzlich diese Übersicht (Suddenly This Overview), 1981, another of Fischli and Weiss's early collaborations, consists of a group of some 250 small sculptures made by the artists from unfired clay — the preferred medium of young schoolchildren (pages 1–7). Among the things presented are a number of surprisingly ordinary and crudely crafted objects as well as a delightful variety of staged vignettes. The series, more specifically, falls into roughly three categories. The first is imagined moments from the lives of famous figures, with such whimsical titles as *Spock is a bit sad that he doesn't have any feelings, Anna O dreaming the first dream interpreted by Freud* (page 2), and *Marco Polo shows the Italians spaghetti, brought back from China, for the first time.* The second contains a group of what the artists call "popular opposites": work and play; theory and practice; high and low (this last, with its possible reference to high and low art, simply presents two dogs — one sitting up, one lying down) (figure 2). The third category presents a selection of everyday objects, among them a loaf of bread, a plate of peanuts, a semi-automatic machine gun (page 107). The physical crafting of the sculptures suggests a sensual pleasure in their making, seemingly confirmed by the sheer variety and volume of the resulting objects. One imagines the pair's thorough engagement in the creation of this mini-universe, both in the actual molding of the pliable clay in their hands and in the conversations that must have carried the project along.

Each object in *Suddenly This Overview* could have grown out of or precipitated a discussion between the artists, running the gamut from the profound to the ridiculous. By pointing this out, I wish to suggest that the spirit of camaraderie existing between Fischli and Weiss, which is markedly different from the solitary working environment of most contemporary artists, is an important component of their work. Their collaboration seems based in large part on the pleasures of sharing their ideas with one another on an ongoing basis. They have been compared, in fact, to the title characters of the great nineteenth-century novelist Gustave Flaubert's last book, *Bouvard and Pécuchet* (1881) — two *flâneurs* (loafers) who, meeting by chance and immediately sensing a kinship of ideas and spirit, form a lifelong partnership. After retiring from their jobs as copyists and moving to the countryside, they spend their time engaged in any number of edifying (or not) diversions and mishaps, all the while pondering questions of the universe, large and small.

Some of the questions Bouvard and Pécuchet might have pondered appropriately appear in Fischli and Weiss's large polyurethane sculpture *Fragentopf (Question Pot)*, 1984 (figures 3–4). One hundred questions line the interior of this oversized, simulated-

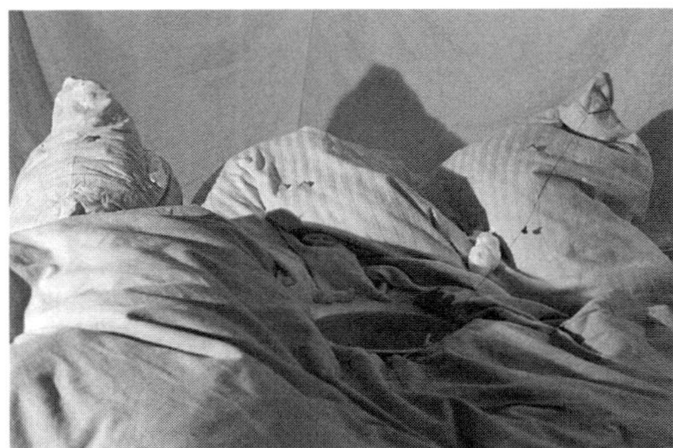

1   *In the Mountains*, from *Wurstserie* 1979
    color photograph

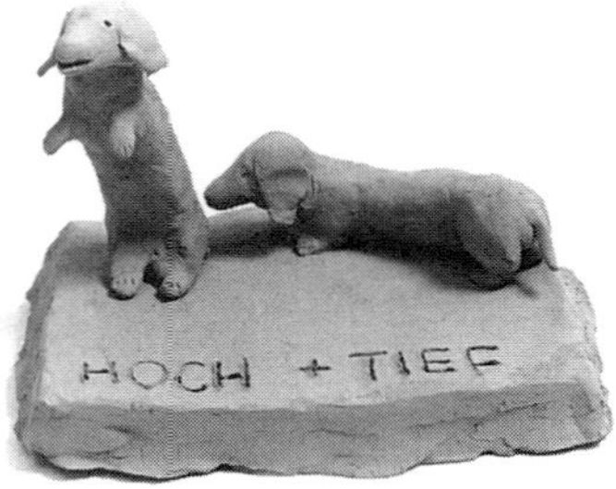

2   *Popular Opposites: High and Low*,
    from *Plötzlich diese Übersicht*
    (*Suddenly This Overview*) 1981
    unfired clay
    Photo: Ywan Schumacher

ceramic pot, which stands nearly four feet high. The object itself, which looks as if it might be more comfortable at a craft fair than in a museum, can be seen as a potshot at the pretentiousness of much late twentieth-century art. Indeed, the artists have expressed their suspicion of art that is overloaded with meaning, something they have referred to in conversations as *Bedeutungskitsch*, or the "kitsch of heavy meaning." Their empathy with ordinary objects may be related, in part, to their distaste for *Bedeutungskitsch*. "We don't think we have a spiritual or philosophical problem," Fischli has said, "and now we must find a way to show it to the world."[1] The viewer who peers inside the *Question Pot* is inevitably engaged by the questions painted inside, a canny mix of the profound and the mundane: AM I NAIVE?; AM I CONNECTED UP WITH EVERYTHING?; WHAT DOES MY DOG THINK?; SHALL I GO TO THE ZOO?; IS IT ALL A QUESTION OF TIME? These questions stimulate both thoughtful meditation and careless hilarity; but, taken together, they negate the possibility of coming to any conclusion, meaningful or not.

Following on the heels of the *Wurstserie* photographs and the *Suddenly This Overview* sculptures, Fischli and Weiss further animated the commonplace in a series of photographs entitled *Stiller Nachmittag (Quiet Afternoon)*, 1984–1985 — often referred to as the *Equilibrium* series — and in the film *Der Lauf der Dinge (The Way Things Go)*, 1985–1987. In the photographs (pages 13–19), such objects as vegetables, kitchen utensils, tires, ladders, chairs, and balloons, precariously arranged, are cast in humorous vignettes with individual titles such as *Nuclear Family*, *The Triumphant Carrot* (page 102), and *Outlaws*

1
Matthew Collings,
"The Stumbling
Objects of
Fischli/Weiss,"
*Artscribe
International,*
November/
December
1987, p. 33.

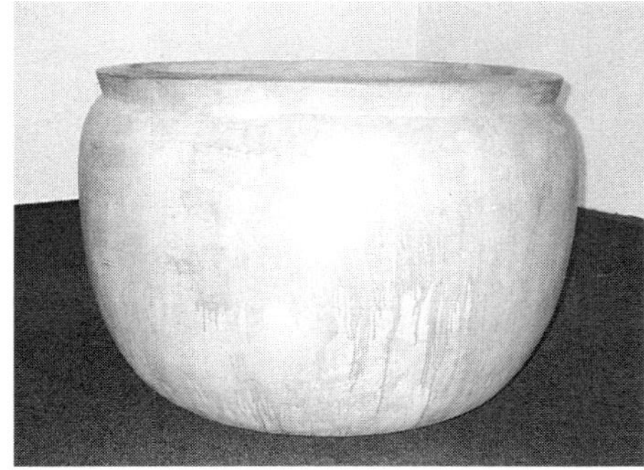
3 *Fragentopf (Question Pot)* 1984
polyurethane, cloth, paint

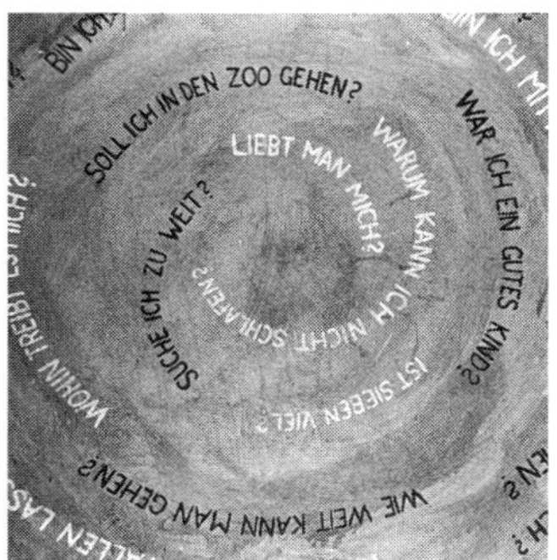

4 *Question Pot* (detail)

(figure 5). In the film (figure 6; pages 28–31), many of these same props are choreographed by the artists into a sustained kinetic slapstick, set in motion with the precision of a Swiss cuckoo clock. A comparison comes to mind with the Swiss artist Jean Tinguely (1925–1991), whose kinetic sculptures, such as *Homage to New York*, 1960 (figure 7), were built to auto-propel into self-destruction. Tinguely's exploding constructions reflect one of the basic tendencies of twentieth-century art: the move toward the dematerialization of the art object. But while Fischli and Weiss share Tinguely's feeling for the evocative potentialities of junk, their film, although constantly on the verge of entropy, never actually succumbs. It might be said, rather, that the artists have restored objectness to their art: the props in *The Way Things Go* are not only the film's protagonists but many have been preserved in two large vitrines (figure 8; pages 32–33). These objects include shoes, teapots, plastic bottles, tin cans, and pieces of lumber that, in combination with fire, gas, and gravity, unfurl in a riveting dominolike processional of controlled chaos. Watching the mesmerizing chain reaction of the film, the viewer is lulled into a childlike fascination with the seemingly endless possibilities for destruction and failure it suggests. These, however, are ultimately avoided by the artists' precise manipulations of their props.

Almost seamless in its final form, *The Way Things Go* actually required months of obsessive preparation and tinkering in a large, poorly heated warehouse space devoted to the project. It is not surprising, then, that shortly after the completion of the film, the artists / *flâneurs* began work on a project that would take them far from the confines of their studio. For the

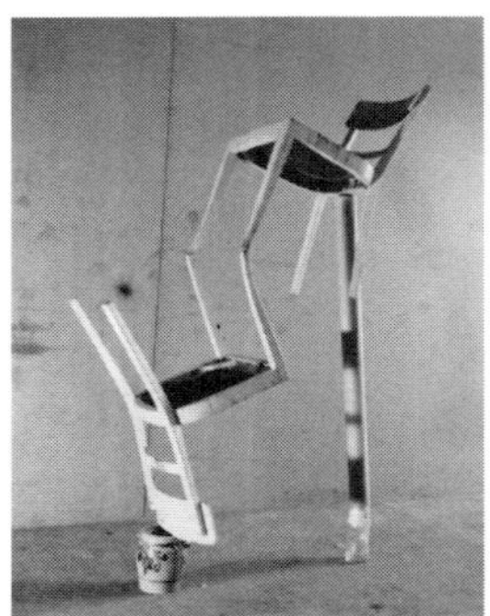

5   *Outlaws*, from
     Stiller Nachmittag
     (Quiet Afternoon) 1984–1985
     color photograph

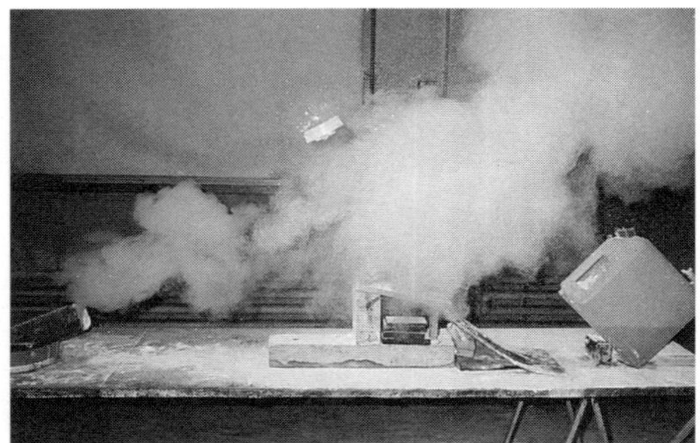

6   *Der Lauf der Dinge (The Way Things Go)* 1985–1987
     16mm film
     Camera: Pio Corradi

series that ultimately became the books *Airports*, 1990 (figure 9; pages 44–46), and *Bilder, Ansichten (Images, Views)*, 1991 (figure 10), Fischli and Weiss took to the road, producing lavish color photographs that, in the end, are surprisingly close to those found in travel agencies — from images of airplanes parked on the tarmac to the most clichéd tableaux of famous tourist sites such as Stonehenge, the Pyramids at Giza, and the Eiffel Tower.

In an article about the *Airports* series, filmmaker John Waters describes the photographs as "mediocre, glossy, postcard-style photos of exteriors of nondescript airports" and "absolutely worthy of a second look." In them, he claims, he has "glimpsed a new kind of 1990s beauty, over and above the banality of pop or the exasperation of minimalism into a shockingly tedious, fair-to-middling, nothing-to-write-home-about, new kind of masterpiece."[2]

The shock of the mundane, of course, has a respected tradition within the history of the avant-garde, dating at least from the exhibition of Marcel Duchamp's early readymades (figure 11), which Fischli and Weiss merrily carry on. Thus the *Images, Views* photographs, like the *Airports* pictures, are provocatively banal. In addition to the famous tourist sites mentioned above, this latter series incorporates such generic and saccharine images as a kitten bathed in sunlight, a tree branch laden with ripe apples, and a butterfly alighting on a thistle. With these groupings of photographs, the artists have created, in effect, their own repository of stock images, largely indistinguishable from commercially made photographs that are embedded in the mass-cultural consciousness.

2
John Waters, "Delayed," *Aperture* 127, Spring 1992, p. 74.

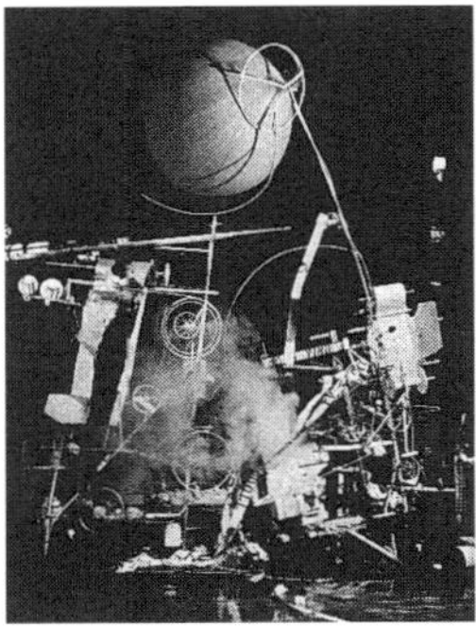

7 Jean Tinguely,
Homage to New York 1960
machine
Collection The Museum of
Modern Art, New York
Photo © David Gahr

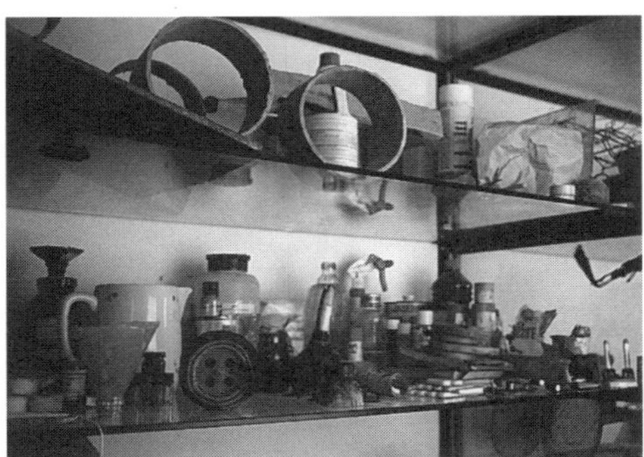

8 Props from *The Way Things Go*

In resurrecting such images, Fischli and Weiss might seem to be engaged in the sort of postmodern critique of the commercial media culture that is so familiar at the end of the twentieth century. Yet, if this is their intention, they do so without the heavy touch of many artists who appropriate media-derived imagery. In its subtle appreciation of the everyday, the *Images, Views* series reflects a more poignant aspect of the artists' interest in making art of the most banal and devalued material of daily life. For it must be remembered that Fischli and Weiss actually photographed each of the images in the series and that in visiting the sites — already known through reproduction — had their own experiences of them. If there is an element of parody in these works, it is comingled with an undeniable spirit of exploration and wonder.

In a work entitled *Le rayon vert (The Green Light)*, also known as *Son et lumière (Sound and Light)*, 1990 (page 34), the artists created a piece that combines two of the more unique aspects of their enterprise: spectacular effects and purposeful mediocrity. This simple construction, which they chose as their contribution to the large, international contemporary art exhibition *Metropolis*, held in Berlin in 1991, consists of a plastic cup, a flashlight, and a turntable. Installed in a dark space, the flashlight is placed behind the plastic cup, which is perched on the spinning turntable, resulting in the projection of delicate patterns of color and light onto the opposite wall. If this work possesses an "oh, wow" effect that is reinforced by the general context of contemporary *Bedeutungskitsch*, it is also, quite simply, an ingenious use of three very ordinary objects.

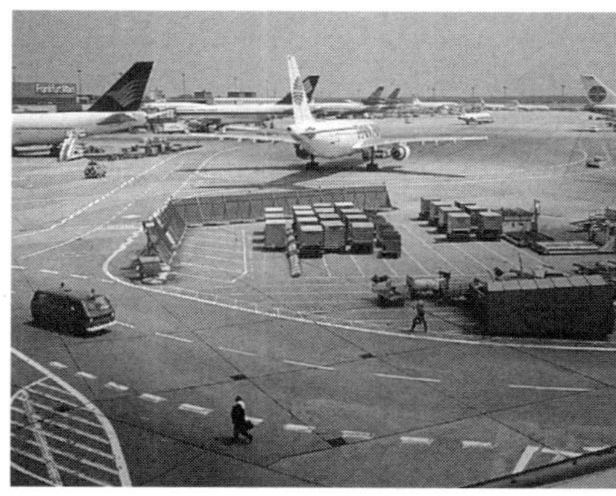

9 *Airports* 1988
Cibachrome

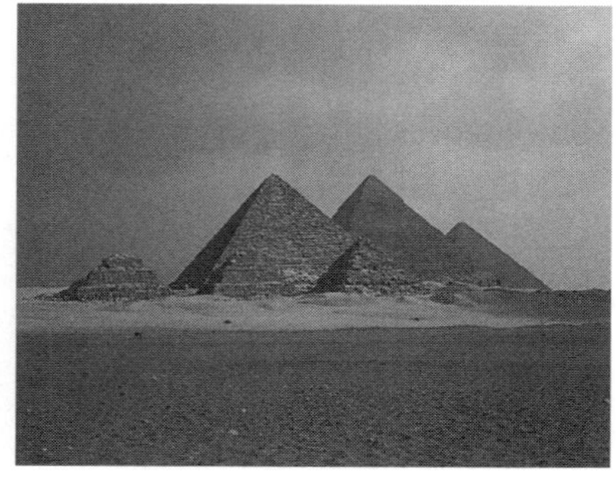

10 *Pyramids*, from *Bilder, Ansichten (Images, Views)*
1991
Cibachrome

The mini-spectacle created by *The Green Light* has been exceeded only, to my mind, by that of Fischli and Weiss's *Kanalvideo (Canal Video)* of 1992 (figure 12; pages 60–61). The video is a readymade, in effect, spliced together from existing footage of the sewage pipes of Zürich. Prior to their discovery of this footage, the artists had long been fascinated by the obsessive workings of their city's sanitation department: one of their favored subjects, made in clay and later in cast rubber (figure 13), has been a pair of sewer workers in the process of cleaning out the pipes. Fischli and Weiss have compared themselves to these workers, who share their engagement with a close examination of society's refuse. However, unlike a good Duchampian readymade — such as the bottle rack, which the French artist hoped would resist aestheticization — Fischli and Weiss clearly relish the dazzling visual effects of their unpromising object. Humble in its origins, this footage is transformed — with a bit of editing and in the authority of the surroundings of the art gallery — into a mesmerizing voyage of color and light, straddling the line between the mundane and the sublime.

The artists' most recent sculptures happen to look a lot like Duchampian readymades, passed through the filter of such mid-century artistic endeavors as Nouveau Réalisme and Fluxus. *Der Tisch (The Table)*, 1992–1993 (figure 14; pages 48, 51), is an enormous table covered with hand-carved and hand-painted polyurethane sculptures that replicate the residue found in the artists' own studio: empty cans, boxes of light bulbs, dirty ashtrays, Styrofoam coffee cups, bits of wood, encrusted paint brushes, videotape containers.

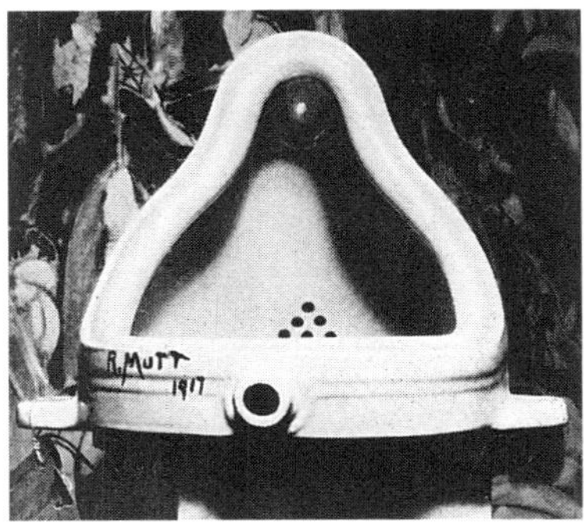

11 Marcel Duchamp, *The Fountain* circa 1917
    black-and-white photograph by Alfred Stieglitz
    Collection Philadelphia Museum of Art;
    The Louise and Walter Arensberg Collection

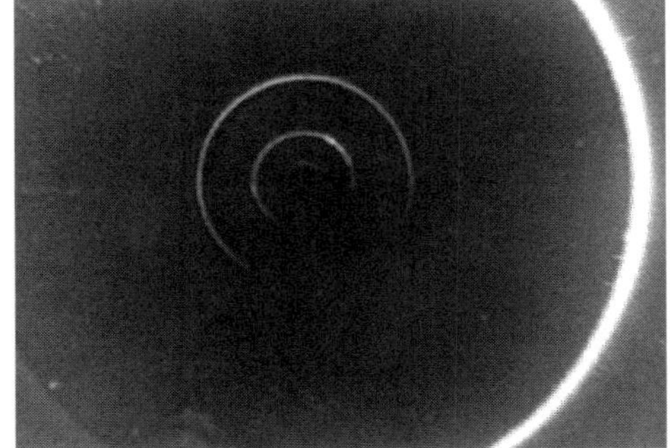

12 *Kanalvideo (Canal Video)* 1992
    video footage of Zürich sewage system canals
    color videotape

3 Excerpt from Dick Higgins's reminiscence of the origins of the Fluxus movement, "A Child's History of Fluxus" (1979), in his *Horizons: The Poetics and Theory of the Intermedia* (Carbondale, Ill: Southern Illinois University Press, 1984).

One can't help but think of the Fluxus credo, "Hey! — coffee cups can be more beautiful than fancy sculptures . . ."[3] or of a Daniel Spoerri *palette d'artiste* from the 1960s, such as *Palette Conny Fischer-Lueg,* 1968 (figure 15). Unlike Spoerri's sculpture, however, which really is made from the remnants of an artist's studio and epoxied in place, the cornucopia of spent materials on Fischli and Weiss's table is a painstakingly handcrafted simulation of what one might find in their work space, where the "still life" is nearly indistinguishable from everyday reality.

The artists have been making sculpture out of polyurethane since the early 1980s. A lightweight, cheap, and highly malleable material similar to Styrofoam, polyurethane has lent itself remarkably well to their various aesthetic permutations. Early on, they worked from large blocks of the stuff, carving low-rent creations such as *Idiot vert (Green Idiot),* 1984 (page 11) that border on the "fantastic." (The artists have described these early polyurethane sculptures as something like a low form of psychedelic experience.) Fischli and Weiss have used the polyurethane to express their sometimes surrealistic tendencies; but by the early 1990s, these pieces had become such close reproductions of reality that they might be more appropriately described as trompe l'oeil. Around this time, they began to make site-specific installations, often in and around museums, which usually took form in existing non-art spaces the artists would occupy and fill with a multitude of polyurethane objects. One such example, *Raum unter der Treppe (Room under the Staircase)* (figure 16), was installed in 1993 in a narrow space under the staircase of the

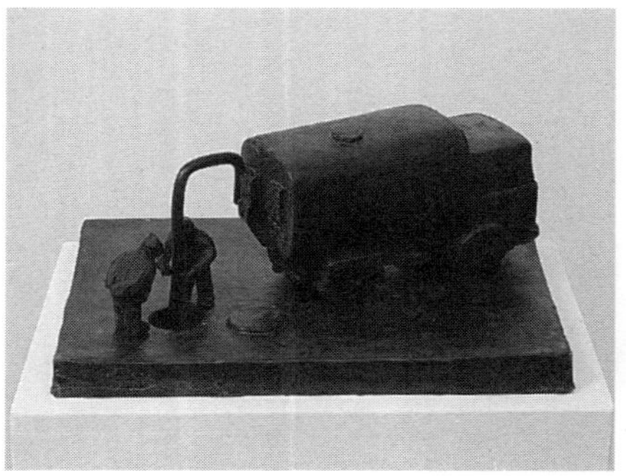

13 *Sewer Workers* 1986
cast rubber, Beracryl

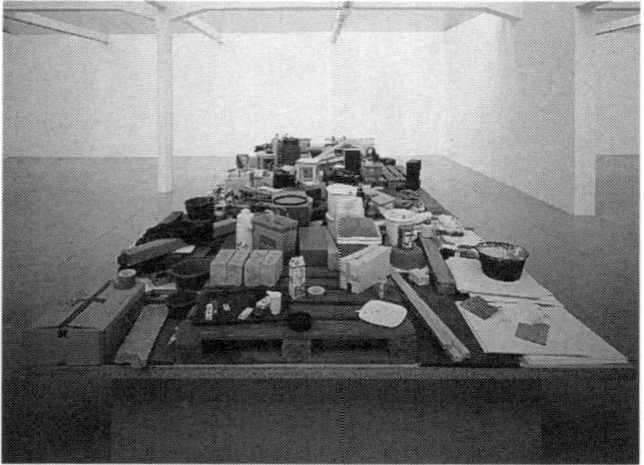

14 *Der Tisch (The Table)* 1992–1993
polyurethane, paint
Photo: Alex Troehler, Zürich

Museum for Modern Art in Frankfurt am Main, Germany. A small window cut in the door allows a glance into what looks like a custodian's storeroom; in evidence are a washbasin, a desk with a phone, a pot of paint on the floor, and any number of miscellaneous materials we might find in the closet of the museum's handyman, including strips of foam rubber, wooden shelf elements, a pair of shoes, and a calendar.[4] The room, an aberrant moment of reality in the context of other artistic presentations in the museum, stands in a nether space somewhere between art and life.

In 1994, the artists made the videotape *Atelier/Bus (Studio/Bus)*, which serves as something of a self-portrait. This subjective-camera video captures the daily routine of the artists, beginning with their commute from home to studio through the outskirts of Zürich and into the city. Once there, we see a work space littered with art tools and supplies, ashtrays, coffee cups—i.e., their everyday paraphernalia, much of which might just be sculptures-in-progress. The videotape briefly holds a shot of an airport, and the viewer is momentarily disoriented. Have we suddenly left the studio? No, the wider focus reveals that this is a photograph on the wall from the *Airports* series. One of the highlights of the video shows the artists (or maybe their studio assistants—we can't see faces) engaged in the act of crafting the inchoate polyurethane into recognizable objects (figure 17). Although the artists may be working with an unorthodox material, their approach is surprisingly traditional. We observe the hands of the craftsmen, diligently sanding the edges of the polyurethane, hand-painting its surfaces, and slowly transforming the material into sculptures indistinguishable from

4
For more information on this site-specific work, see Jean-Christophe Ammann and Rolf Lauter, *Peter Fischli/ David Weiss, Raum unter der Treppe* (Frankfurt am Main: Museum für Moderne Kunst, and Stuttgart: Cantz Verlag, 1995).

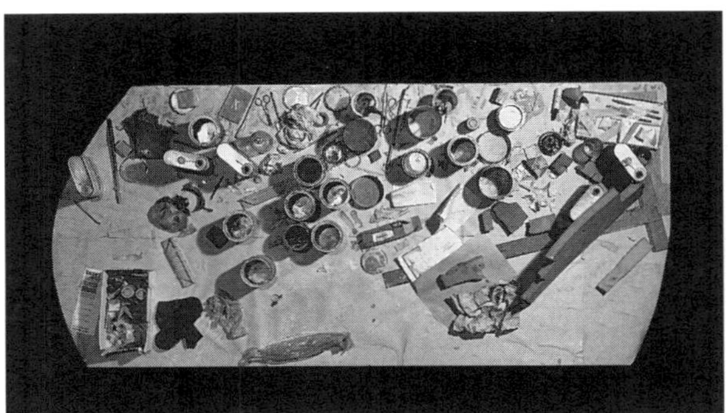

15 Daniel Spoerri, *Palette Conny Fischer-Lueg* 1968
mixed media on wood
Collection Museum Boymans-van Beuningen, Rotterdam

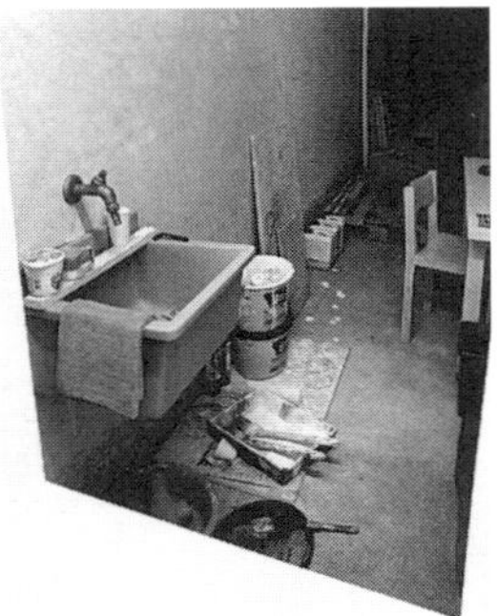

16 *Raum unter der Treppe*
(Room under the Staircase)
1993
polyurethane, paint

objects in the studio. Ironically or not, high-art techniques are applied to mundane materials in order to replicate prosaic objects. One suspects that the artists take real pleasure in the laborious and time-consuming crafting of these objects themselves, not to mention in making art that simulates objects of so little conferred value.

The *Studio/Bus* video spawned an ambitious installation involving ninety-six hours of videotape, shown on twelve monitors, that was premiered when the artists represented Switzerland at the 1995 Venice Biennale (figure 18). In the epic scope of its anti-epic subject matter and imagery, and in its sprawling presentation, this project is akin to the first *Suddenly This Overview* installation. The Venice videos are no more and no less of an "overview," and they reflect yet another aspect of the artists' evolving interest in ordinary aspects of daily existence. For the Venice project, they each chose subjects that were of interest to them, including the chef at work in their local restaurant and the annual motor-cross races, not to mention workers from the local sanitation department (page 66). A number of the Venice videos were shot outdoors, especially in the mountainous regions of the Alps around Zürich; they often include long shots of what Goethe once called "the laughing Nature." Fischli and Weiss gave their days over to the videotaping and, as they worked, they allowed the camera to follow visual elements of interest often unrelated to their ostensible subject, a working process they characterize as a form of "concentrated daydreaming." In this mode, for instance, they might allow the camera to linger idly at a window in the background as they — momentarily transported by the effects of the light through the glass — allow the video to follow its own course.

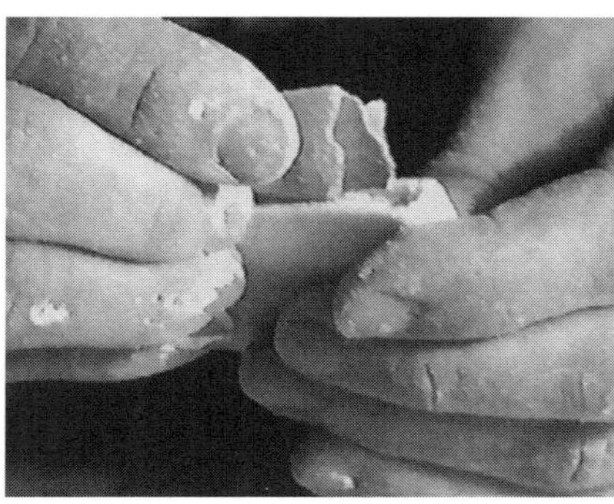

17 *Atelier/Bus (Studio/Bus)* 1994
color videotape

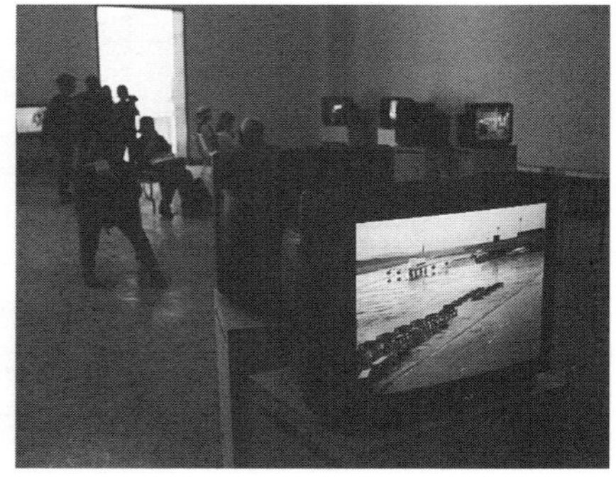

18 Video installation at the Swiss Pavilion,
Venice Biennale 1995
Photo: © Mancia/Bodmer

This almost passive attention given over to the details of everyday life, whether prosaic or spectacular, is initially disconcerting. The viewer might wonder where the videos are leading or question the meaning behind the artists' decision to use their time in this way. One of the aspects of Flaubert's novel *Bouvard and Pécuchet* that Fischli and Weiss claim to have particularly enjoyed was the spectacle of two grown men spending a great deal of time making useless things. The idea of "misusing time" (Fischli and Weiss's term) — especially in a culture that puts a premium on the work ethic and the constructive use of time — gives the artists great satisfaction.

Yet, for them, generating the Venice videos was less a conceptual exercise (say, in the spirit of Warhol's filmmaking) than a primal experience comparable to that of the Lumière brothers who, under the thrall of their invention of the moving image, found themselves enraptured with this new medium's capacity to capture everyday life. For early film audiences, as for the Lumières themselves, the first filmed image of the world was equally enthralling; it was like discovering the world anew. My sense is that Fischli and Weiss wish to convey this same spirit of wonder in their Venice videos, as if we haven't slowed down and really looked at the world around us in a lifetime of distractions. (Boris Groys's essay in this volume addresses this topic in greater depth.) Running in real time, with no clearly demarcated beginning or end, and largely uninflected by the artists, these videos look extraordinarily ordinary. As such, they present a challenge to spectators. To fully experience the piece, viewers would have to "misuse" a good deal of time, as the artists themselves have done. It is time during which they are not asked to meditate on the state of the world, on their own state of mind, or on the state of art today — although any of these speculations are warranted — but simply to let the mind wander at will.

The earliest museums of the sixteenth and seventeenth centuries were sometimes called *Wunderkammern*, or "wonder cabinets," and the term "museum" originally referred to a spot dedicated to the Muses, "a place where man's mind could attain a mood of aloofness from everyday affairs."[5] In a century that has seen notions of modern progress give way to cynicism and a distrust of the future, Fischli and Weiss have fixated on another loss: our capacity for wonder. On some level, Fischli and Weiss's art reflects their own desire to regain this capacity, so diminished at the end of the twentieth century. The viewer who becomes engaged in their art shares the artists' pleasures in the everyday sublime of our time and place.

5
Lawrence Weschler, *Mr. Wilson's Cabinet of Wonders* (New York: Pantheon Books, 1995), p. 27.

FISCHLI

WEISS

PLAY / THINGS

For Chloe, play had always meant make believe. In the absence of any dolls, the child Chloe dressed her mother Sasha's dinnerware in linen napkins — the spoons and forks were women; the knives men — and spun out great family sagas with criss-crossed plots unfolding over the course of days, or even weeks.

Rebecca Goldstein, "The Geometry of Soap Bubbles and Impossible Love." [1]

In an effort to identify an aspect of common human experience that is in some way akin to artistic creation, Freud once turned to childhood play: "Might we not say," Freud asks, "that every child at play behaves like a creative [artist], in that he creates a world of his own, or rather, rearranges the things of his world in a new way which pleases him?" [2] I begin a discussion of Fischli and Weiss with this citation from Freud because their oeuvre seems to fall into two main kinds: one in which they do, indeed, as in the spirit of play, rearrange the things of their world in new ways which please them; and another kind (still, as we shall see, in the spirit of play) in which they allow the things of their world to stand unrearranged, presenting transcriptions of reality so uninflected by their presence as to raise in an aggravated form the question of what makes it art. There is an intermediate genre as well, in which the artists fabricate objects that have the *appearance* of things in their world; but these objects are then arranged cunningly to look as if they have been placed where they are without premeditation, and hence appear radically unrearranged. Here, an uninteresting answer to the question of what makes it art is that it is imitation, which is all that one famous theory of the nature of art requires.

But at this early stage in my discussion there is no great urgency to be taxonomically exhaustive. For the mode of play to which the two main genres of Fischli and Weiss's work correspond is not, I think, the one Freud exactly has in mind in his essay. This, after all, was written at a moment — 1907 — when it was not altogether thinkable that there should be art even distantly similar to the kind Fischli and Weiss produce (the readymades of Duchamp, for example, or a film like Warhol's *Empire*). Or at least it was not thinkable from within what we might call the "art world of Freud," which consisted, near at hand, in

1
Rebecca Goldstein, *Strange Attractors* (New York: Viking, 1993), p. 163.

2
Sigmund Freud, "Creative Writers and Daydreaming," in *The Standard Edition of the Complete Psychological Works of Sigmund Freud*, vol. 9, ed. James Strachey (London: Hogarth Press and Institute of Psychoanalysis, 1959), pp. 143–153.

I use the expression "creative artist" where Freud uses the expression "creative writer." He is thinking about poets in the essay, but I cannot suppose this widening of reference in any way modifies his analysis. If Freud held a view in which the visual artist is an *imitator* of reality and the poet a *creator* of an imaginary reality, that distinction could hardly have survived reflection.

the small-scale antiquities he collected with such zeal, and, in the farther distance, in the tremendous works he visited on holiday — the Moses of Michelangelo, say, or the Virgin and Saint Anne of Leonardo. And this tends to skew Freud's reading of childhood behavior (on which, as a psychologist, he might have been thought authoritative), largely because he leaves the notion of what pleases the child insufficiently analyzed. So while I take my departure in this essay from Freud's idea of play, I must proceed to subvert it by drawing attention to a different, very familiar form of play that is quite close to the spirit in which I regard it instructive to think of the work of Fischli and Weiss but which, nevertheless, is quite at odds with the kind that concerns Freud.

Freud's model of play is one in which "the opposite of play is not what is serious but what is real." Such play is serious because the child *takes* it seriously, but it is not "real" in the respect that the child, in Freud's analysis, is only pretending: pretending to be doing what grown-ups in fact do. He argues that a child's play is determined by a certain wish, "the wish to be big and grown up." Hence, "the child is always playing at being 'grown up' and in his games he imitates what he knows about the lives of his elders." In the world according to Freud, little girls play with dolls and miniature articles of furniture, thus imitating the nurturing and housekeeping that Mama, as model, really does. And little boys build towers and knock them over in what they imagine to be Papa's life in the real world of construction and deconstruction. A child, then, is an imitation adult in Freud's psychology in just the same way in which the fetus was a miniature adult — a homunculus — in the obstetrical schemes of the Middle Ages, where we see fully formed men and women in medical illustrations of the uterus. Children's play, according to Freud, is make-believe adult behavior, executed with miniaturized adult paraphernalia known as toys. Freudian play is imitation work. At this point it is worth interjecting the thought that if there were an overall wish animating the work of Fischli and Weiss, it would be the inverse of the child's wish, according to Freud: it would be the wish to play as children play — but hardly if, as Freud says, the child is driven by the wish to be grown-up![3]

Freud's image of children's play is that it is a rehearsal for adult life, and no doubt there is a species of this sort of play. But it hardly seems a rehearsal for the life of the adult creative artist, which, after all, Freud had promised to help explain. Such play furthermore contrasts vividly with the kind of play described by Rebecca Goldstein in the passage from

3

Since, according to Freud's theory, the *pleasure* of childhood play is the pleasure of imagining oneself as really doing something real, this pleasure must altogether abate when one really does something real, as an adult. But Freud, always fertile in generating ideas, had a further theory (which I shall not go into deeply here) that we might call the Principle of Hedonic Conservation: "The growing child, when he stops playing, gives up nothing but the link with real objects: instead of *playing*, he now *fantasizes*. He builds castles in the air and creates what are called daydreams." Freud's picture of adult life is not pretty: work gives pleasure only when imagined by the child; so when we put aside childish things, we must find other fantasies and be driven by wishes other than to be effective and grown-up. It doubtless says a lot about Freud that he seems to find no room for pleasure in work itself; but, after all, the Biblical explanation of why we work is that it is a form of punishment for an original disobedience.

one of her stories I cited above. I refer to a form of make-believe in which the child does not so much imagine she is an adult, let alone wish she were a grown-up, but rather makes believe (for example) that spoons and forks are women and knives are men in scenarios in which she herself may have no role at all: she remains outside the play, like a prime mover.

Chloe herself is an invention, of course, in which the writer doubtless made believe that some individual in real life played as a child the way Chloe does. The story Goldstein tells about Chloe thus belongs to the same genre of make-believe as that in which her character indulges. What is striking about Fischli and Weiss is that they have preserved this form of play (which each of us knows from childhood, even if we are far from having been the virtuosi of make-believe Chloe evidently was), and they have carried it intact into adulthood in the form of art. I say "carried it intact into adulthood" in order to make clear that there would be something quite literally childlike in their play even if it could be argued that *all* of art is somehow continuous with this species of play. For very little art seems so conspicuously to exhibit the inventiveness of childhood play theirs does as it transforms knives, forks, and spoons into mountaineers and acrobats or uses pots and automobile tires in such a way that they appear to have wills of their own. The creativity exemplified in such bodies of work as their *Wurstserie* of 1979 or *Stiller Nachmittag (Quiet Afternoon)* series of 1984–1985 — or in their spectacular film *Der Lauf der Dinge (The Way Things Go)* of 1985–1987 — answers to the same impulse as the kind of food-and-table play in which every child participates. Thus in their artwork there is, along with a tacit impudence (for one expects art to be more "serious" and less obviously a form of play), a certain sweetness and a kind of innocence, even if it transcends in its complexity what children themselves are able to do. Even in that portion of their work in which things of the world are left resolutely unrearranged there is an extraordinary purity in the banal scenes they favor in their depictions, which are untouched by squalor or obscenity.

Chloe was fortunate in the fact that her mother "had been too charmed by the dramas of the spoons and the forks to spoil anything by providing Chloe with real dolls." For a lot of childhood play — food play, for example, or playing with the family flatware — is calculated to drive parents crazy, and so it has a touch of the politics of insubordination about it. It provides the child a way of being provocative and bad. There remains a question of the *degree* to which the politics of childhood is carried forward in Fischli and Weiss's art,

4
Bice Curiger, "Sunday Children," in Bice Curiger, Patrick Frey, and Boris Groys, *Peter Fischli David Weiss*, exh. cat. (Venice: XLVI Biennale di Venezia, and Bern: Bundesamt für Kultur, 1995), p. 35.

5
Marcia E. Vetrocq, "The Birthday Biennale: Coming Home to Europe," *Art in America* 80, no. 9 (September 1995), p. 77.

but one cannot help but feel it is essential to their enterprise that, as with children, it is done primarily for each other's approval and entertainment, possibly with one eye cocked to see if anyone in position of authority is annoyed.

It had to have been immensely gratifying, then, when someone in the art world, which today commonly accepts anything as art, actually should have grown vexed and impatient with their work at the Swiss Pavilion at the Venice Biennale of 1995 — ninety-six hours of video recording shown on twelve monitors (enough footage and monitors, in any case, to guarantee that viewers would be hard-pressed to take it all in, even if they spent an entire eight-hour day seeking to do so) of expeditions undertaken by the two artists, possibly edited to remove the suspicion of anything faintly interesting. Where Bice Curiger, supportive from the beginning, wrote poetically of the artists' "predilection for the inconspicuous wonders of everyday life,"[4] Marcia E. Vetrocq complained in *Art in America* that Fischli and Weiss "seem to be making at least four boring points" with their video footage of banality squared.[5] But the Swiss Pavilion work belongs to the second kind of Fischli and Weiss's work, the kind that consists in the unrearranged presentation of the world, the bare repetition of things as they are. This has, perhaps, as its closest weapon in the armory of childhood behaviors, the act of mimicking — always infuriating, even if, or especially if, the child apes the adult exactly, adding nothing of his or her own to the parents' authoritarian blather. The work of unrearranged banality — photographs of things everyone knows, which show them just as they appear in photographs intended to show them just as they are known — raises complex questions to which I will return later. In the meantime, however, it is worth observing that the "four boring points" Vetrocq supposes Fischli and Weiss to be making (among them, "art offers no resolution") are almost certainly not points intended by the artists.

Play as analyzed by Freud requires toys that are simulacra of objects in the adult world: tools, for example, blunted in order to enable children to play at being grown-up and productive without hurting themselves or straining their limited strength; pails and shovels for the sandbox; toy stoves and plastic dishes for the girl's room; toy cars for the boys to crash and popguns to make them manly and brave; dolls to activate maternal instincts; lead soldiers to activate leadership; stuffed animals to give boys and girls alike a model of passive softness in those with whom they will sleep. Of course, there are toys of other sorts — games, athletic gear, and the rest — which have the function of socializing the child into adult patterns (a responsibility sufficiently important to have made the manufacture and purveyance of toys a serious and profitable business). Most of these toys, needless to say, also afford the child plenty of opportunity for generating annoyance: squabbling over whose turn it is, making a racket, creating messes, hitting one another over the head, refusing to share, etc. Still, most toys that are manufactured and distributed through commercial outlets such as Toys 'Я' Us have fairly defined functions, which parallel their functions in adult life and thus fit Freud's theory of play nicely.

These kinds of toys contrast with the vastly more creative case of making toys out of things that were designed to play an altogether different function, such as using a sausage, whose function is to be eaten, as a motor boat or racing car by pushing it around the table and saying Vroom vroom vroom or Putt putt putt. Or sticking a fork, like a mast, into a baked potato and displaying it to Mommy as a sailboat. Whatever the politics of such transformational gestures, there can be no question but that they exemplify the kind of creativity Freud *ought* to have been considering. The child who turns wurst into a sports car or speedboat is not imitating a worker on the assembly lines at Ferrari but instead has engaged in something close to a magical or metaphorical transformation. The child has taken something out of one complex of instrumentalities — out of what Heidegger designates the *Zuhandene* (the ready-to-hand) — and given it a fresh, if momentary, identity as something very distant from it in another complex of instrumentalities altogether, over which he or she exercises total effective control. The child is able to do this because it sees in the smooth, elongated, and sleek curvature of the wurst a shape morphologically analogous to that of a racing car, and in so doing, effects what I have called the "*is* of artistic identification,"[6] declaring the wurst to be a racing car by playing with it as if it is one. This is one way of being a creative artist. To be sure, the parents are less likely to see the act under this description than under the no less true description "playing with food" — an act that carries something of the strong interdiction that belongs to spilling seed in the Biblical code of the forbidden.

The *Wurstserie* (pages 22–23), which consists of photographs of metaphorically transformed *wurstwaren*, is the first work in the long collaboration of Fischli and Weiss, and it is a perfect example of transformative play by grown-ups whose glee in arranging scenes

6

In "The Art World," *Journal of Philosophy* 61, no. 19 (1964), pp. 571–584.

for each other's pleased approval is transparent. They have used sausages as improvised toys and to considerable effect—in part because the sausage is an inherently comical comestible and, at the same time, because it participates in the seriousness of food. For after all, the chief purpose of adult work is to put food on the table. At the very least it displays a disrespect for work, as well as a profound ingratitude, to play with it, that is, to put it to what the adult sees are unserious ends. The sharing of food is a ritual of the deepest importance in family life; it is when the family comes together to be affirmed in its unity and restored in its being by what work has put on the table. It is altogether fitting that the meal be sacralized by the voicing of grace, a thanksgiving for the daily bread and the fruit of labor. So eating is hedged about with taboos and meanings that the child who plays with food transgresses. And the parent who enjoins the child not to engage in such food play is endeavoring to reinforce the system of meanings that defines family life. The child already understands enough of these meanings when he or she plays with food to appreciate the action as insurrectionary. And since the kind of play the scenes of the *Wurstserie* exemplify are, at a simple level, metaphorical transformations of the kind that, at least primitively, define art, it would be difficult to imagine a work in which the relationship of art to society as conceived by Fischli and Weiss could be better displayed. They subvert meanings and violate taboos—but it is still only play, as the comedy of the wurst guarantees. It is like the moral argument of *Paradise Lost* as conceived by boys and girls sophisticated in the heavy ceremony of the Swiss dining room.

Imagine, if you will, the evening meal, composed of cold cuts. Sister picks up a wurst, looks at her brother in complicity, and says: "Here is Fräulein Wurstli. And here"—wrapping a slice of mortadella around Fräulein Wurstli's dubious waist—"is her pretty petticoat!" Little Brother, not to be outdone, responds in kind—"Here is Fräulein's sports car"—as he distributes little roundels of salami for wheels around the wurst he should be eating rather than playing with, as Mother and Father quickly make plain. The constructions in the *Wurstserie* photographs enact the ceremony of the *abendmahl* (evening meal) as defiled in house after house in Zürich and elsewhere in Mittel-Europa by what Curiger felicitously designates "Sunday Children." The artists are grown children who remember the fun (what Freud would call "pleasure"). "Look, this sliced bologna looks just like a pile of little rugs!" Fischli or Weiss says. "Why not make a rug store?" Weiss or Fischli responds. No sooner said than done: little stacks of sliced bologna in various formats are distributed as in a salesroom. "We need some customers," one of the pair observes, and perhaps some cigarette butts are pressed into service for the role, so long as their height is small in proportion to the diameter of the "rugs." "We'll call it *In the Carpet Shop!*" (figure 1) they cry out as one. Were it not for the figures, it would look like a sparse display of cold cuts. Without the title it would look like a sparse display of cold cuts with some small vertical objects, like cigarette butts. As photography it is neither here nor there. As art it is perhaps less powerful than the political structure of play that gives it its energy and the meat that gives it comedy.

But in time the *Wurstserie* presses against the boundaries of something stronger. (Not that the artists necessarily want to transcend the boundaries that determine their project.) It was a passing thought of Socrates that the underlying structures of comedy and tragedy are of a piece, and in some way that goes quite beyond what one might suppose sausage capable of, scenes in the *Wurstserie* take a dark turn. In *The Accident* (figure 2), which has the uncanny look of an Expressionist painting, two *wurstwagen* have collided at the intersection of two narrow streets, formed by buildings made of cardboard cartons into which windows and doors have been cut. A number of spectators in the form of cigarette butts stand about or look onto the mishap from their apartment windows. One of the vehicles has lost a wheel, and a victim lies on the street, "tossed like a cigarette butt" from the wreckage. In *The Fire of Uster* (page 23)[7] the box-buildings have been set afire, the street is strewn with wreckage, and one of the sausages appears to have landed, like an airplane far too silly to have done such harm, in the fateful intersection. The image is extremely

7
It is tempting for the non-Swiss to misread the city of the title as Ulster (as I originally did). Fischli and Weiss explain that Uster is a suburb of Zürich where in 1832, in a rare incidence of Swiss insurrection, a factory was set afire, possibly by the workers.

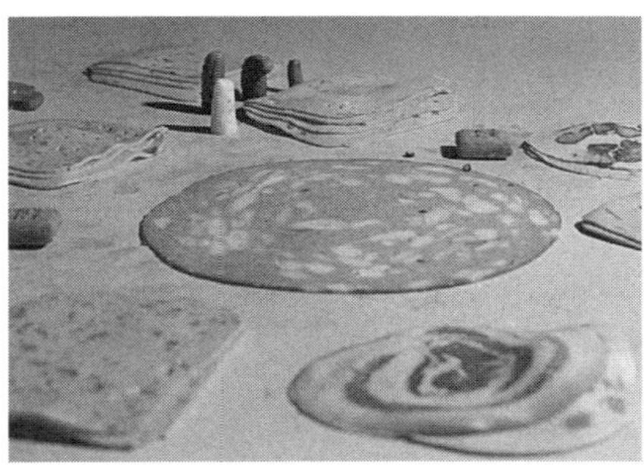

1   *In the Carpet Shop*, from *Wurstserie*   1979
color photograph

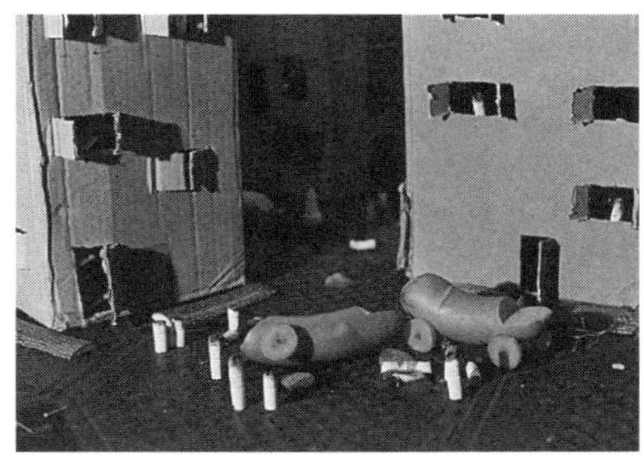

2   *The Accident*, from *Wurstserie*   1979
color photograph

convincing, which demonstrates the power of play and imagination, even when exercised on the most unlikely materials.

The concept of play comes through with particular vividness in the *Stiller Nachmittag (Quiet Afternoon)* photographic series (pages 13–19).[8] Although there remains a certain amount of food play (here with potatoes and carrots), one has the impression that two children have sought to break the boredom of a quiet afternoon by engaging in a kind of balancing contest, using kitchen utensils with the vegetables, to see who can come up with the most audacious arrangements. These are acrobatic still lifes, generally modest in scale but animated by titles that anthropomorphize the equipoised components and turn them into peers of the pieces in Calder's *Circus*. Thus in *The Triumphant Carrot* (figure 3), a grater and two pieces of tableware interact with four carrots to form a pair of tumblers, one of whom, on his (or her) back, legs in the air, balances the other. In another piece called *Honour, Courage, Confidence* (figure 4), the flexibility of a compass saw is exploited to form a springboard, on the end of which a wine bottle stands with a singular verticality, preparing to take the plunge. And in the marvelous assemblage of *Roped Mountaineers* (figure 5), some graters, a spatula, a carrot and fork, and what ought to be a Swiss Army knife, if it is not one, form a team of mountaineers, roped together as they climb a particularly scaly slope.

These pieces have the improvised and spontaneous appearance of three-dimensional equivalents to doodles, as when one balances a pencil across one's coffee cup to make time pass at a boring meeting. But they transcend doodles because of the personifications the

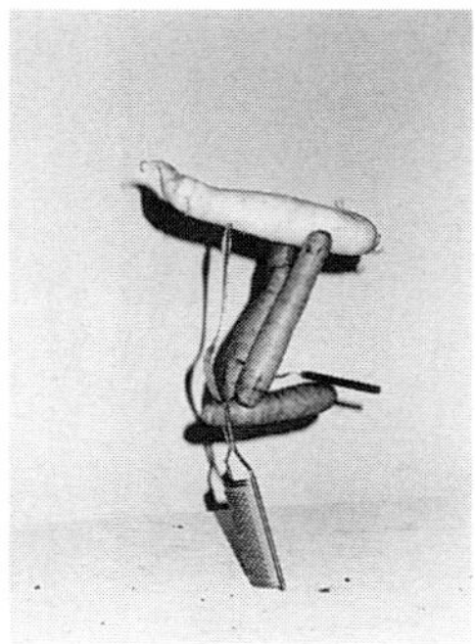

3 *The Triumphant Carrot*, from
*Stiiler Nachmittag
(Quiet Afternoon)*
1984–1985
black-and-white photograph

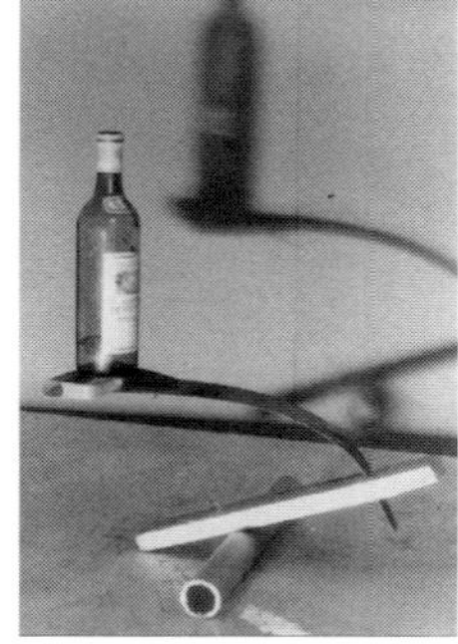

4 *Honour, Courage, Confidence*,
from *Stiiler Nachmittag
(Quiet Afternoon)*
1984–1985
black-and-white photograph

titles suggest and because of the comedy that accompanies the idea of brave bottles and triumphant carrots. The need to maintain the balance induced upon their components suggests danger, but of a kind that is perhaps inconsistent with the *unfall* (accident) that haunted the scenes of the *Wurstserie*: if the "mountaineers" fell in a tangle of cord, they would simply revert to their identity as mere utensils. To induce an accident onto the delicious *Ben Hur* (figure 6)—a chariot made up of a pan balanced on wheels that are spools of scotch tape, pulled by a "horse" that is also balanced on a spool and made of what appears to be an aerosol can—there would have to be a wreck that would just look like a pan, some spools, and a can. The play at times outgrows the scale of mere toys, as when Fischli and Weiss balance tires (figure 7) or even kitchen chairs in precarious arrangements, giving the latter the interesting title of *Outlaws* (page 15). Daniel Soutif[9] relates Fischli's account of how the compositions always collapsed after a few brief moments, provoking the artists to question how they might utilize the energy of these breakdowns. This led, via the intervention of genius, to their masterpiece, *The Way Things Go* (which I would prefer to translate as "The Course of Things"), a film in which tires and scuffed wooden chairs play a starring role (figures 8–10; pages 28–31).

The film consists of a number of events linked together in an improbable causal chain: a rotating garbage bag untwists the rope from which it hangs, moving closer and closer toward the floor as it does so until it touches a tire positioned beneath it, which now takes up the action by rolling down an inclined plane and banging into a plank that gives it a further kick, which initiates a stepladder's awkward descent until it trips, which causes a further reaction . . .

9
Daniel Soutif,
*"Der Lauf der Dinge
ou la causalité
sauvage,"*
in *Peter Fischli
David Weiss*,
exh. cat.
(Paris: Centre Georges
Pompidou, 1992),
p. 23.

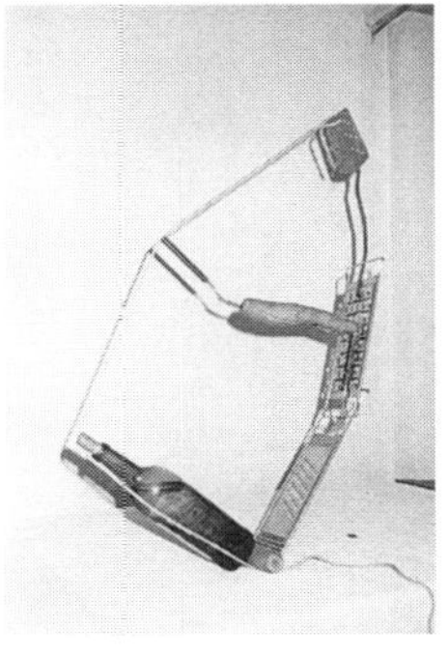

5   *Roped Mountaineers*, from
     *Stiller Nachmittag
     (Quiet Afternoon)*
     1984–1985
     black-and-white photograph

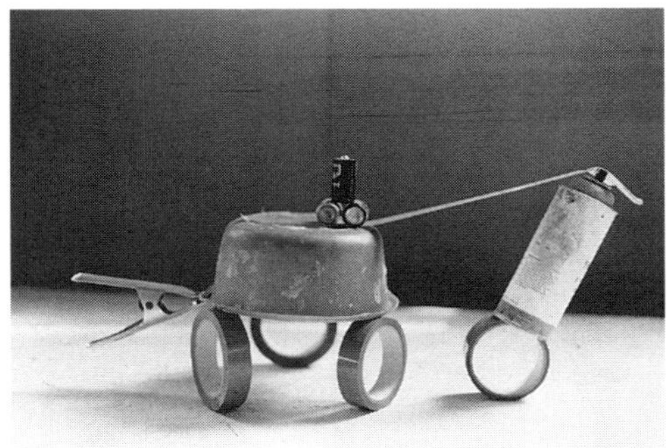

6   *Ben Hur*, from *Stiller Nachmittag (Quiet Afternoon)*
     1984–1985
     black-and-white photograph

10
In fact, the film is highly constructed (i.e., edited). It was filmed over a long period of time, after many trials and errors in producing the individual cause-and-effect sequences.

until, ultimately, some sort of inflammable foam goes up in smoke as it spills over the lip of a tray. Between start and finish, more tires are set rolling, bottles are overturned, liquids spill, and things ignite, untwist, explode, rotate, and roll on eccentric axes along dinky tracks.

As is often observed, the film has the deflected ingenuity of a cracked inventor such as Rube Goldberg, who drew such contraptions for his readers' amusement a generation or so ago. But there is this difference: Goldberg's contrivances were madly complex devices, requiring an improbable assemblage of components for achieving tasks capable of being done by anyone simply and directly — like lighting cigars or rocking a baby or pouring coffee. They were caricatures of so-called Yankee ingenuity, expressing itself in "labor-saving devices" that "no home should be without"; but, rickety and crazy, these devices interposed so much mediating gear between agent and task that one always feared they would not be up to the homely demands made of them. The causal chain in *The Way Things Go*, on the other hand, has no function and no goal. But in concatenating slides, rolls, tumbles, spills, booms, bangs, and spins, it vividly illustrates what Kant offers by way of characterization of the work of art: it seems purposive while lacking any specific purpose. It does nothing, but it seems to embody, for viewers to whom I have shown it, meanings that touch on waste, violence, pollution, exhaustion, and despair, all somehow reinforced by the overwhelming sense of suspense generated by the fact that it is a film: the individual episodes seem to happen one after another, smoothly and without interruption — the danger being that something will go wrong and break the chain.[10] It is, for all

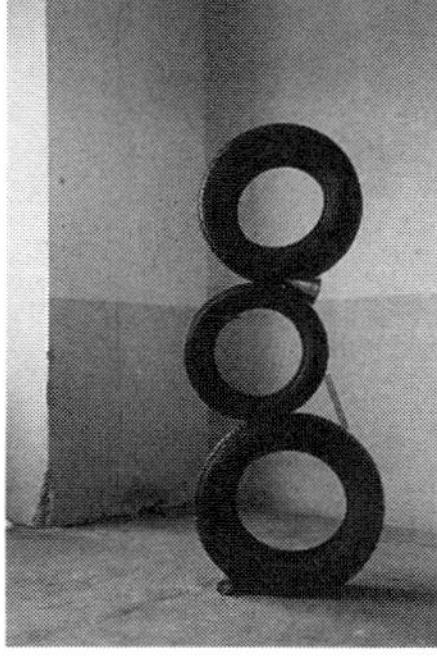

7 *Untitled*, from
*Stiller Nachmittag
(Quiet Afternoon)*
1984–1985
black-and-white
photograph

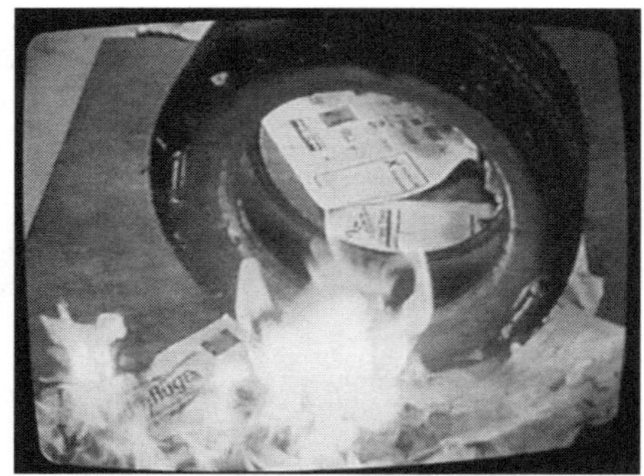

8 *Der Lauf der Dinge (The Way Things Go)* 1985–1987
16mm film
Camera: Pio Corradi

the triviality of its individual episodes, an epic of some kind, vastly transcending the connotations of play while retaining the spirit of innocent mischief in which boys at play egg one another on to high and higher efforts which, taken collectively, seem to imply the pointless horror of unending war. Beginning with a Katzenjammer Kids mentality, Fischli and Weiss take their mischief to a distance so great that the resulting work becomes a postmodern classic, with a rich art-historical pedigree ranging from Jean Tinguely, the fabricator of self-destroying machines, to Joseph Beuys, who made art of soap, old newspapers, and whatever was, to echo Heidegger once again, "at hand."

The tremendous difference between the two photographic series I touched on earlier and *The Way Things Go* is that the latter, in Heideggerese, stresses the thingness of the things it uses and does not treat them as metaphors for something else. *Ben Hur*, for example, sees the possibility of chariotness in a plain cooking utensil. Part of the pleasure of the work consists in the way the pan continues to be just what it is and yet, for purposes of play, has become a chariot (just as the tape spools, remaining mere tape spools, have turned for purposes of play into wheels). The objects in *The Way Things Go* remain what they are throughout. In many cases, to be sure, they are deflected from the uses for which they were invented. The tires do not cushion any vehicles or rim any wheels, and yet they do what enables them to serve their purposes when attached to vehicles: they roll. But they also get filled with liquid, like tires left out in the rain. And, in at least one somewhat scary episode, they go up in flames (figure 8), the way the tires filled with gasoline and hung

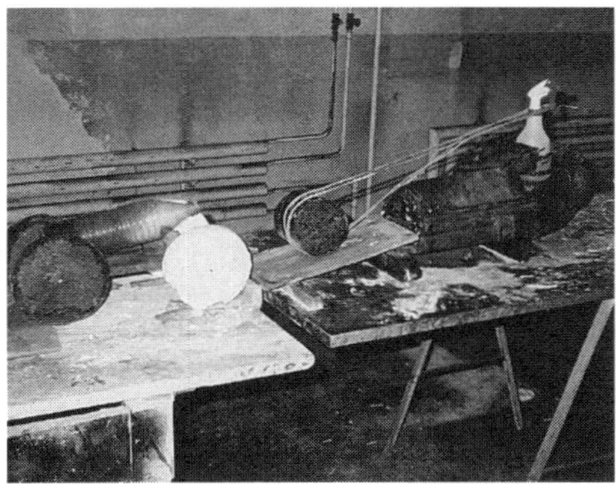

9   *Der Lauf der Dinge (The Way Things Go)*
1985–1987
16mm film
Camera: Pio Corradi

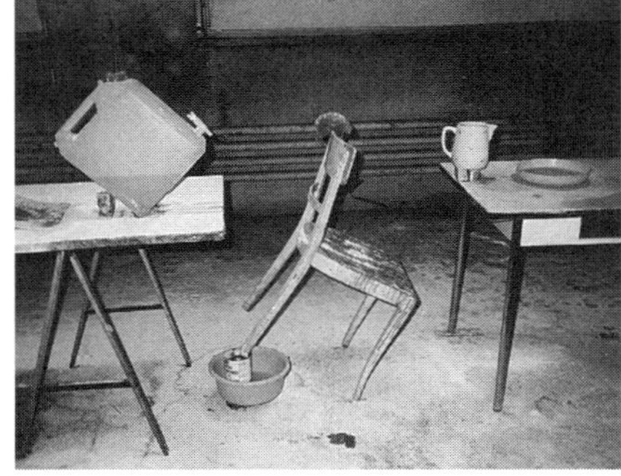

10   *Der Lauf der Dinge (The Way Things Go)*
1985–1987
16mm film
Camera: Pio Corradi

round the necks of suspected traitors as "necklaces" do in acts of Third-World retaliation. Indeed, in the grunge and squalor of the space in which the causal chain is enacted, with all the flames, ropes, racks and tracks, treacherous slides, and dripping water, there is something of the air of the interrogation space, where information and screams are pried out of victims by means of flames, ropes, racks and tracks, treacherous slides, and dripping water. It is this analogy, perhaps, along with the suspense, that gives the film its uneasiness and its moral edge.

And those hard wooden chairs (figure 10)! We have seen them in the scenes of torture by the painter Leon Golub in which victims, bound and blindfolded, are tormented with clubs and lighted cigarettes (figure 11). (This validates the vocabulary of the *Wurstserie*, in which cigarette butts, all at once a symbol of cruelty, stand in for human beings.) And when Bruce Nauman inserted a straight chair into a piece of sculpture (figure 12) this, too, was widely read as a reference to torture. The chair tipping over in **The Way Things Go** seems at once comical and frightening, as it would be if someone were sitting in it tied up. Perhaps this is why viewers do not always laugh, are not sure whether this is funny, are uncertain what the response is supposed to be. If there is a moral, perhaps, it is that once detached from the wheels that give them their use and for which they were designed, tires can find a range of deflected applications — from improvised hoops to cheap and convenient instruments of torture and incineration. And chairs can become the vehicles for torture. This is an argument for each thing having its place in a well-run society, which is the positive side of celebrating (if that is what it is) banality.

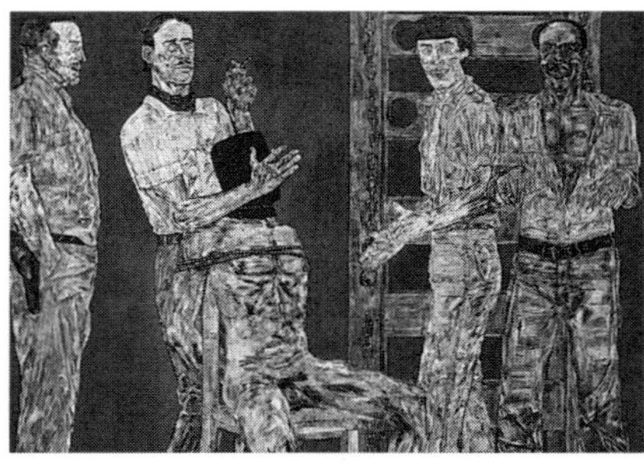

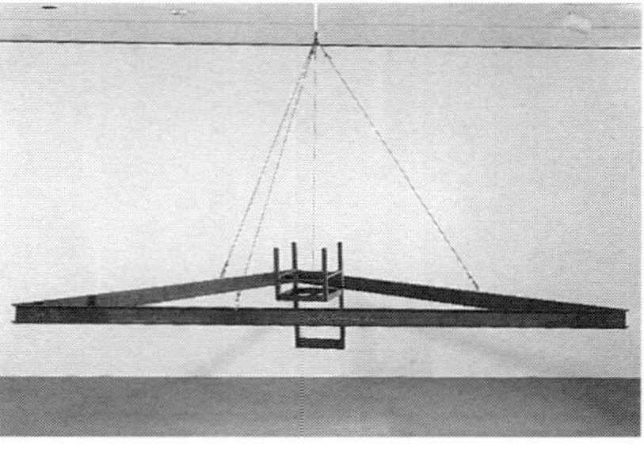

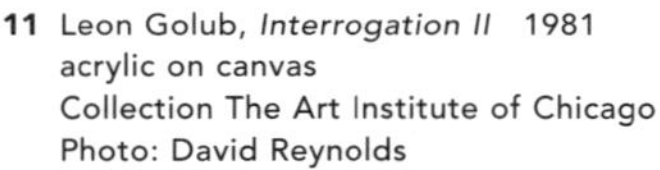

11 Leon Golub, *Interrogation II* 1981
acrylic on canvas
Collection The Art Institute of Chicago
Photo: David Reynolds

12 Bruce Nauman, *South America Triangle* 1981
welded steel beams, cast iron chair
Collection Hirshhorn Museum and Sculpture
Garden, Smithsonian Institution, Washington, D.C.;
Holenia Purchase Fund, 1991
Photo: Lee Stalsworth

Between the *Wurstserie* and *Quiet Afternoon* series, Fischli and Weiss produced a work with the sardonic title *Plötzlich diese Übersicht (Suddenly This Overview)*, 1981 (figures 13–14; pages 1–7), which consists of some 250 small objects in clay that inventory the world understood as an aggregate of things. The title of the work is an expression that might come out of the mouth of someone who, like the archer in the *Bhagavad Gita*, is vouchsafed a vision of the entire universe. There is a certain wit in the association between the mystical expostulation of the title ("All at once I see everything!"—as if in response to the Lord Krishna's stunning self-disclosure, "Behold my forms . . . by hundred and by thousands, of various sorts")[11] and the stumpy objects in fact, kneaded into recognizable shapes rarely aspired to in sculpture: a car driving past trees along an autobahn, a woman in a supermarket, a junk yard, some *tchotchkes*, a pot, a loaf of bread, a housing project, a waste truck for some men cleaning sewers — a world of *dinge* that includes in its neutral, enumerative phenomenology an automatic rifle.

An early paper by the American philosopher Willard van Orman Quine carries the title "On What There Is," and it begins as follows:

> A curious thing about the ontological problem is its simplicity.
> It can be put in three Anglo-Saxon monosyllables: "What is there?"
> It can be answered, moreover, in a word—"Everything"—and everyone
> will accept this answer as true. However, this is merely to say
> that there is what there is. There remains room for disagreement over cases:
> and so the issue has stayed alive down the centuries.[12]

11
The Bhagavad Gita, XI, 5, trans. Franklin Edgerton (Cambridge, Mass.: Harvard University Press, 1972).

12
W.V.O. Quine, "On What There Is," *Review of Metaphysics* 2, no. 1 (1948), pp. 21–38.

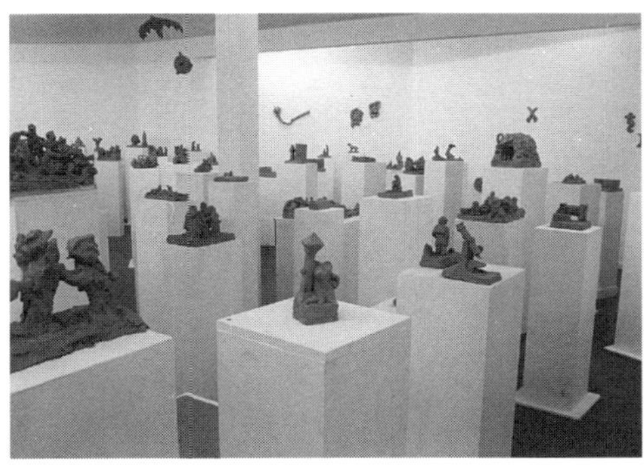

13 *Plötzlich diese Übersicht (Suddenly This Overview)* 1981
unfired clay objects

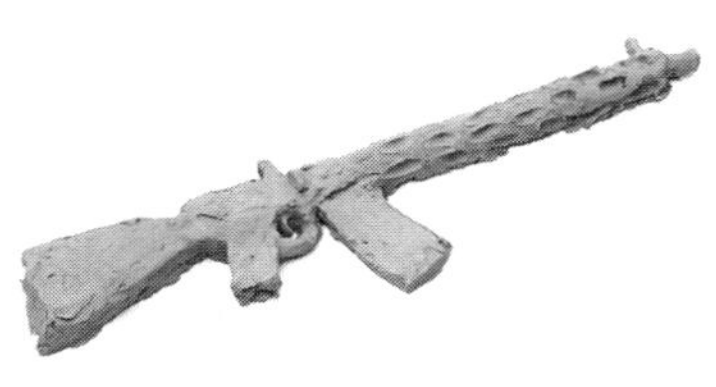

14 *Semi-automatic machine gun*, from *Plötzlich diese Übersicht (Suddenly This Overview)* 1981
unfired clay
Photo: Ywan Schumacher

Quine's little metaphysical dialogue gives a philosophical edge to *Suddenly This Overview*. It is as though the work were an attempted answer to the question of what there is. It is an effort to put everything into clay: the autobahn, the supermarket, the kitchen sink, the housing project. "Don't forget bread," one can imagine one of the artists saying. "Or guns," the other one responds, each turning the words into clay deeds. If nothing else, the work shows the limitations of images by contrast with words: "Everything" has a sweeping total simplicity in contrast with its messy translation into every thing.

Notwithstanding the little clay gun, this is not a work with a political subtext, as near as I can make out. There is again a certain sweetness about the work, as there is about its statement, if we see the latter in the framework of philosophy. It is the answer a child might give to the Ontological Question. The answer has a touching concreteness. There is nothing scientific pictured in "Everything"—no positrons, muons, genes. There are simply shovels and loaves of bread, stubby cars and the kinds of buildings ones sees on the outskirts of towns everywhere. It is the world as everyone lives in it, the world of dailiness, the world of common experience, the dear, predictable world anyone who knows the world of *The Way Things Go* longs for. Such a person would give anything for a glass of fresh water, some dry socks, a warm meal, roads not potholed by mortar shells, gas stations where the pumps work. On the news last night, there was gas in the kitchens of Sarajevo for the first time in half a year. The answer may not be metaphysically deep. But morally, humanly speaking, there is no answer deeper.

In *Suddenly This Overview* there is something of the spirit of Pop, which, a generation earlier, also undertook to effect a reconciliation with the ordinary—with the things everyone knew and understood, with the world that critics of the common culture dismissed as hopeless and banal. There is, of course, a difference here, in surface if not in spirit, inasmuch as Fischli and Weiss do not, in this work at least, make an effort to effect exact simulacra of ordinary objects, in the manner in which Warhol did with the Brillo carton (figure 15) or the Campbell's soup cans. They did this, to be sure, in the curious subgenre I remarked on early in this essay, in which they replicated the most ordinary of ordinary objects in carved and painted polyurethane. Commentators have proposed a certain affinity—that treacherous concept!—between these later works and the readymades of Marcel Duchamp (figure 16). But, in fact, the sole resemblance between the two is that it was a condition of the readymade that it be an object of ordinary life of no redeeming aesthetic value, and the objects imitated in polyurethane are likewise objects, like cans of paint or candy wrappers, of no redeeming aesthetic value. From that point of intersection, however, the works by Fischli and Weiss proceed in a direction utterly different from the one Duchamp took.

In truth, these works by Fischli and Weiss have a very ancient pedigree: they are essentially exercises in trompe l'oeil, where the ordinariness of the objects that deceive is a condition of their success in deceiving. But neither deception nor illusion was a factor in the philosophical intention of the readymade, which spurned perception altogether. The readymade was rather an effort to diminish the importance of aesthetics, and hence of beauty, in the assessment of works of art. The Pop object did not spurn aesthetics at all: Warhol found the Coca Cola bottle as beautiful and as reassuring as he found the Mona Lisa. Fischli and Weiss's objects are not engaged in that polemic. They simulate paint cans and place them where one might expect to find paint cans. And so, like the ancient Greeks, they aspire to a kind of cognitive prank — an illusion that really is in the spirit of play, in the spirit of the wallet attached to a string which the pranksters pull the moment someone bends down to pick the wallet up. It little matters that the wallet itself is carved and painted polyurethane.

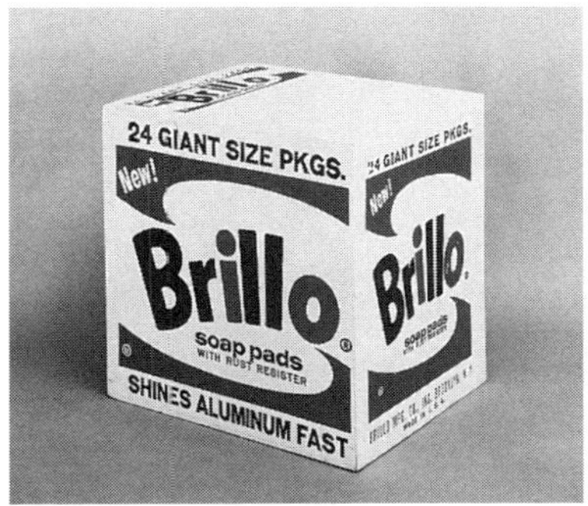

15 Andy Warhol, *Brillo Box* 1964
synthetic polymer paint and silkscreen ink
on wood
Courtesy The Andy Warhol Foundation,
New York

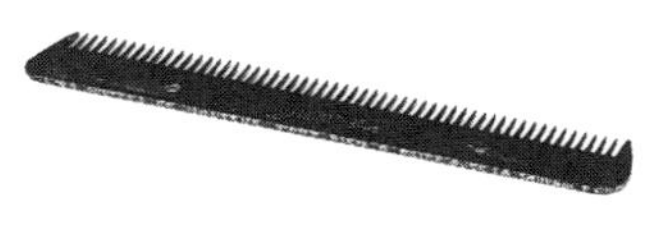

16 Marcel Duchamp, *Ready-made Comb* 1916
steel comb
Collection Philadelphia Museum of Art;
The Louise and Walter Arensberg Collection
Photo: Graydon Wood

13
Boris Groys,
"Simulated
Readymades
by Peter Fischli/
David Weiss,"
Parkett,
no. 40/41 (1994),
pp. 33–37.

There is, I add parenthetically, an artworld prank that the existence of readymades makes available to Fischli and Weiss. Believing the artists have used actual paint cans as readymades, the connoisseur picks one up only to be ontologically disconcerted by the lightness of the cans, which look real but feel fake.[13] It is this duplicity that enabled their work to play a pivotal role in a pathbreaking exhibition at the Kunstverein of Cologne in 1994, titled by its curator, Udo Kittelmann, *Der Stand der Dinge (The Condition of Things)*— a tribute to *The Way Things Go.* The exhibition consisted of things that were not works of art; things that, though in every physical respect indiscernible from things of the first sort, *were* works of art; and then works like Fischli and Weiss's, which looked like things but in fact were polychrome polyurethane. You could not tell to which category these last works belonged by looking at them, but only by picking them up, which made them less radical than the readymade but more mischievous, and in a way more vexing for the theoreticians who classified them as imitation readymades when in fact they were imitations *tout court* — but of things rarely imitated in art because of their robust commonplaceness.

Consider, for example, the singular installation of Fischli and Weiss's work at the Sonnabend Gallery in New York in 1994 (figure 17) against the background of the ancient contest between Zeuxis and Parahesios, as recounted in Pliny's *Natural History*. Zeuxis removed the veil from the painting he had made of a bowl of grapes, so cunningly executed that the gullible birds of Athens converged on the painting and began pecking away: the usual story. Parahesios, asked to remove the veils from his painting, said that the veils were painted and hence were the painting; and he was the better artist since, while

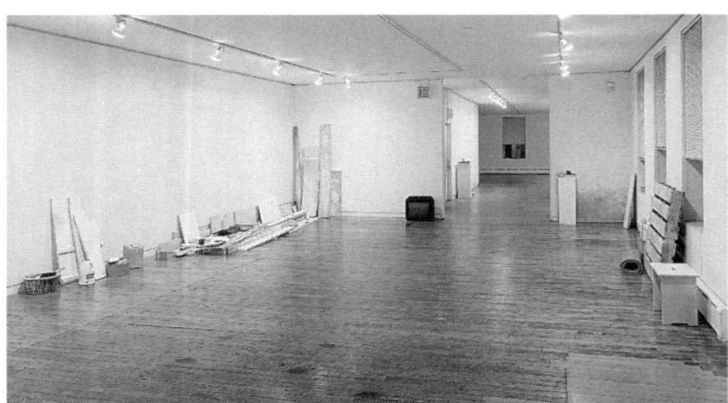

17 Installation view at Sonnabend Gallery, New York   1994

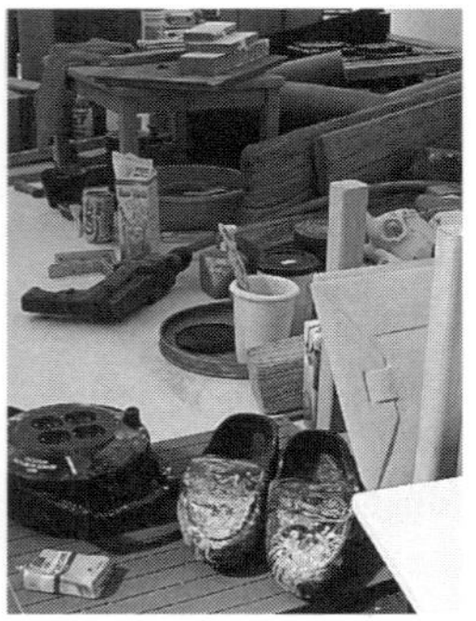

18 *Der Tisch (The Table)*
1992–1993 (detail)
polyurethane, paint

Zeuxis had fooled mere birds, he had fooled rational beings like us. One walked into the Sonnabend Gallery expecting to see an exhibition and instead saw the sorts of gear whose presence one might associate with the installation of an exhibition: spools of tape, Elmer's glue, mat knives, electrical plugs, tubes of caulking, and the ubiquitous coffee cup in waxed blue paper with an appropriate Greek motif, as if a clue. There were stepladders, ashtrays, buckets of paint and plaster, and some small power tools such as electric drills. There were some boards and brushes. One immediately assumed one had come either too early or too late, but in fact this *was* the show! The objects were in polyurethane, carved and painted by Fischli and Weiss as sons of Parahesios. The illusion worked because one immediately inferred to the best explanation of why these objects were there — a show was being installed — just as the judges on that long-ago day inferred to the best explanation of the draperies — that there was a painting behind them. Once the illusion had been lived through, one could enjoy the ingenuity or the accuracy, or even criticize the show for having left something out. It would in any case not have been in celebration of the ordinary so much that these objects were fabricated in the Fischli/Weiss studio, but that the objects themselves were of a kind so embedded in common life (in the common life of the art gallery, in this case) that the inference to the best explanation inevitably yielded illusion. Of course, there was something of a pointed contrast between life and art here in that one does not ordinarily see effigies of paint trays and rollers in an art gallery as art. But neither were the Greeks especially prepared to see drapes as art when illusionistically depicted. The point is that there was a context, subverted by the art, in which drapes would have a natural place and a ready explanation.

The element of illusion is inseparable from at least the initial experience of a group of works executed in rough contemporaneity with the Sonnabend show. *Der Tisch (The Table)*, 1992–1993 (figure 18), for example, again in painted polyurethane, is a three-dimensional still life, as abundant as the painted still lifes of the Dutch masters of the seventeenth century of a fishmonger's stall or a table piled high with fruit and flowers, only here composed of the familiar plastic containers of everyday life: orange-juice cartons, Ajax boxes, soft-drink cans, cups, basins, cans, glue bottles. Seen in a gallery, the best explanation is that this is a scene of real work, that the worker is away for a moment, and that the mess will all be cleared up when the work is done — an explanation that yields to the proposition "The mess is the work" and the conclusion that one is looking at art. *The Table* has as its affinities the figures of Duane Hanson or even the puddle of plastic vomit Sue Williams used in one of her installations on the theme of eating disorders, except, of course, that the message of Fischli and Weiss is relatively benign. They seem clearly to love the clutter of the everyday world of work, with its brightly colored commercial products, and they have found a way of making art out of it. It has, indeed, the same interest as art that it would have as reality, only from the perspective of the anthropology of everyday life.

The recent photographs and videos are more complex because they are less complex. They show the world of everyday life in its everydayness, virtually without comment (and thus belong to that genre of their work in which the things of the world are left unrearranged). Consider the photographs from the series *Airports* (pages 44–46). These are pictures of the kind given out with boxes of Swiss chocolate or as collectors' items in those round containers of wedges of Gruyère. They could be readymade photographs, I suppose, but in fact they were made by the artists to simulate the zero degree of photographic artlessness. But they are real photographs, nonetheless. To attain conceptual parity with the objects in the Sonnabend show, these photographs of airports would have to be paintings done so skillfully as to look like commonplace photographs, photographs so artless and obvious that there is nothing to say about them. But what's the point? Why not just show the photographs, which make whatever point they make about the world, and forget for the moment about art? (For whether they have been appropriated or simulated is immaterial; it is impossible, in this case, to determine the difference empirically.)

One photograph shows an Air France plane (figure 19), drawn up to the jetway. All about are the baggage wagons, the gasoline trucks, the vehicles we never see except at airports, and here and there a worker on the tarmac. It could hardly be more uninteresting as a scene, or as photography, or as art. But as *The Way Things Go* makes manifestly clear, ordinary objects have their dark side, and the bland peaceful world of orderly routine, which facilitates the conduct of ordinary life, is achingly fragile. Who can look at an Air France plane through the security of a window in the airport and not think of the seizure by desperate hijackers of an Air France plane on the tarmac not so long ago, and of the agony of men and women who, embarked on the most ordinary of ordinary errands — taking a commercial flight for business purposes or pleasure — are thwarted and terrorized by the intervention of political violence into the world defined by the system of inferences that yield the "best explanations" in the illusions we just spoke of?

I am always moved by the words of the French mystic Maria Bashkirtseff, a beautiful woman who died young. She had been inculcated with a mystical philosophy in which there were assurances of a higher reality and of the world itself as a distraction from the true pursuits of the enlightened soul. At the moment of her death she cried out, *"Maman! Maman! C'était pourtant si beau la vie!* (Mama! Mama! How beautiful life was, *even so*)."* That *pourtant* is fierce and powerful. In the end I think of this tremendous utterance when I see these works of Fischli and Weiss. In *Suddenly This Overview* there is a little clay figurine of two of the Rolling Stones, Mick Jagger and Brian Jones, walking home with their guitars (figure 20). The title is: *Mick Jagger and Brian Jones Going Home Satisfied after Composing "I Can't Get No Satisfaction."* It is a somewhat sophomoric idea, at which one winces or smiles, depending upon how indulgent one feels. I can imagine a pair of figurines, a lumpy self-portrait, of the artists trudging home with the camcorders they used for the Venice footage. The title of it would be "Peter Fischli and David Weiss Going Home Thinking How Extraordinary the Ordinary Is after All, Having Put It on Videotape as Ordinary as It Is." The ordinary acting on the ordinary can produce art! The innocence of the work carries over into the innocence of this revelation.

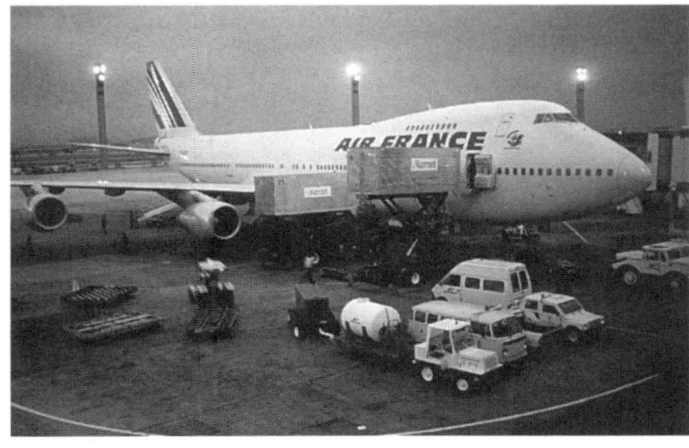

19 *Airports* 1989
Cibachrome

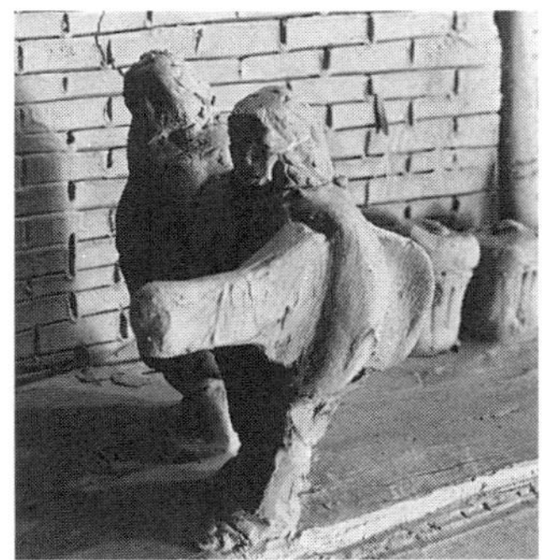

20 *Mick Jagger and Brian Jones Going Home Satisfied after Composing "I Can't Get No Satisfaction,"* from *Plötzlich diese Übersicht (Suddenly This Overview)* 1981
unfired clay

THE SPEED OF ART

Art has achieved an unparalleled speed in our century. I am not talking about the representation of speed in art, an issue that was explored by the Futurists, for example, but about the speed with which art is produced. It was primarily Duchamp's readymade technique that dramatically increased the speed of art. Today it is enough for an artist to look at and name any chosen fragment of reality in order to transform it into a work of art. In this case art production has virtually achieved the speed of light. The readymade technique is probably the greatest technical achievement of the twentieth century next to the splitting of the atom, if you take speed as the decisive criterion. This acceleration guarantees today's visual arts a certain cultural rank and authority, which become apparent on comparing the speed of producing pictures with, for example, the speed of producing texts.

But the increased velocity of art is also considered a menace and kept in check, just as one would not want to deploy the atom bomb. The history of the fine arts after their acceleration at the beginning of this century is the history of their deceleration. The most effective damper on the speed of art is the modern criterion of newness. Not everything that can be declared art is actually acknowledged as such. We expect the artistic gaze to show us something new, that is, something that has not yet been filed away in existing archives. Since these archives keep getting fuller and since the public does not always have the grace to accept deviations from things seen before as something new, art production is of necessity curbed by the need to be new. The economy of innovation checks the rampant growth of art. Thus, the demand for novelty slows art down instead of speeding it up. When compared with existing archives, most of what is produced as art—or rather, envisioned as art—is found to be tautological, redundant, superfluous, and therefore rejected. But art is not always to blame. Sometimes art moving at the speed of light is simply too fast for its innovations to be registered as such. As they go racing by, the outside world often sees nothing new in these innovative deviations—they seem to be too small, too inconspicuous, too vague—and dismisses them. Artists would therefore be well-advised to keep themselves in check and to synchronize the speed of their art with the tempo of real life. That way, others will be better able to perceive and understand them.

Fischli/Weiss have always been great brakemen. They slowly and laboriously carve objects out of polyurethane that have a disarming resemblance to readymades, instead of simply picking them out of reality with the above-mentioned speed of light. The artists have apparently adjusted to the ordinary speed of handcrafted work and come closer to life's sense of time. But there is a hitch: their deceleration is imperceptible from outside because the carved objects look exactly like actually selected readymades (figures 1–2). Thus, Fischli/Weiss simulate readymades by hand — a procedure that inverts the conventional practice in our industrial age of simulating handcrafted work by machine.

As always in such cases, the reasons for this inversion are many. But one thing is clear: this strategy allows the artists to exhibit readymades without being exposed to the criticism that their work is not new, because making readymades by hand is new even — or rather especially — when no one notices it. Fischli/Weiss thus sidestep the deceleration effect imposed on the speed of their art by the demand for novelty. They can quote anything they please from real life with uncensored serenity, as long as they go to the effort of replicating it by hand. The decelerated process of producing art, on one level, thus allows Fischli/Weiss to increase the speed of their art on another, much more important level. And this increased velocity in turn gives the artists the privilege of enjoying things that would otherwise have been sacrificed to the censorship of innovation. This also applies to their videos of outings presented at the Venice Biennale.

What deserves our attention? And what doesn't? Among the thousands and thousands of images with which we are bombarded, which ones shall we choose as valuable and which ones shall we discard as worthless? And according to what criteria? Fischli/Weiss are

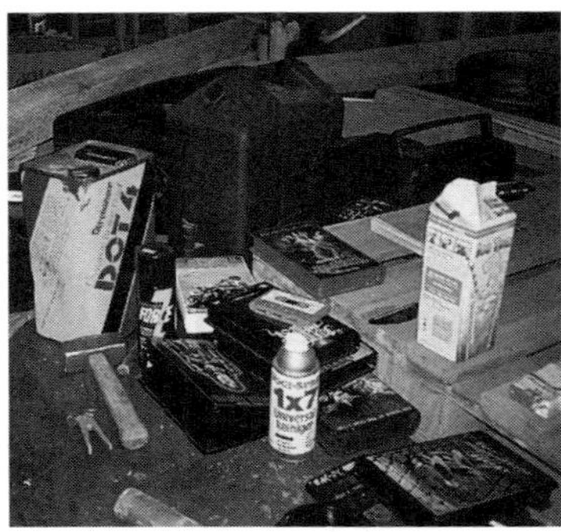

1   *Der Tisch (The Table)*   1992–1993 (detail)
polyurethane, paint

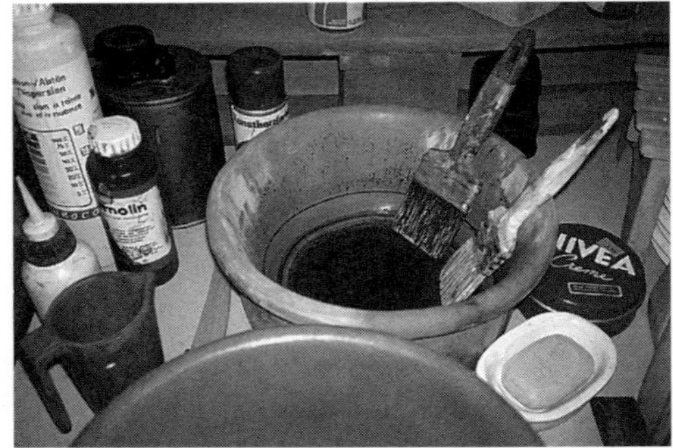

2   *Der Tisch (The Table)*   1992–1993 (detail)
polyurethane, paint

particularly vulnerable to this uncertainty in selecting pictures because central to the issue of the readymade, a long-time concern, are the criteria for selection.

Pictures may be attractive, romantic, picturesque, gloomy, suggestive, or strange. But none of these qualities are acceptable criteria for the professional artist. Artists need new pictures, never seen or shown before, that do not fit in any cubbyhole. They can let the pictures pass mental review — which is a very speedy affair. But the uncertainty remains and paralyzes the determination to make a decision. If something is imaginable, then it can't be new; it is by definition trivial, dispensable. The speed of the imagination runs headlong into a dead end, where it is consumed by the agony of making a choice. Fischli/Weiss step on the brakes just in time.

In their search for pictures, the artists drive through Zürich and its environs or sometimes through different, more distant places and cities, filming things on their way. Then they stop and get out, take walks, visit various places, watch and film what is going on there, and drive back to Zürich again, filming the landscape on their way home. Cars are fast, as Marinetti has observed. But not as fast as the imagination and the gaze. Nor as fast as conventional film and video montage. While the speed of pseudo-readymade production was adjusted by Fischli/Weiss to the tempo of handcrafted manufacture, their new video works are marked by a sense of time that evokes civilized leisure, unrestrained, contemplative enjoyment of time with no outside pressures, undefined, detached curiosity, relaxed recreation after work or on weekends. And once again, it is the increased speed of their art that allows Fischli/Weiss to simulate the leisurely pace of unpretentious human existence.

The slow pace of the Fischli/Weiss excursion videos is, incidentally, not generated by artistically decelerating the tempo that now seems "normal" to us in films and videos, and that corresponds to our daily confrontation with the medium of television. Increasing or decreasing the tempo that is typical of television productions is currently the most common artistic device in the making of "art" films and videos. As a rule, a video or film production with artistic intent can be spotted immediately because time flows faster or slower than it does on television, or perhaps even in circles, through the constant repetition of certain scenes. But when Fischli/Weiss make videos of their outings, they are simulating the readymade sense of television time. Nor does the look of their pictures contradict the television viewer's conventional aesthetic expectations. There is nothing particularly "artistic" about the images; they are not distorted in any way, nor do they show any of the traits of "home movies" that often characterize art videos.

Instead, they cultivate the look of perfectly "normal" television aesthetics, in other words, precisely the look that current video art is trying to subvert in its quest for new pictures. The result is the now familiar effect of the accelerated speed that characterizes the "production" of readymades. "Art" videos have to be short because it is an effort to invent, produce, and look at new pictures: every one of those "creative" video works involves a long, time-consuming, laborious, and difficult quest. But videos that act like television are relatively easy to produce and multiply. And they are easy to watch. This gives Fischli/Weiss a surplus of time, which means that they can produce a great deal within a relatively short period. This surplus time — not regained as in Proust, but simply won — might in fact be read as the underlying theme of the excursion videos. The traditional aesthetics of the readymade using objects and single pictures was never able to fully exploit the surplus of time because inevitably restricted exhibition space put a limit on speedy multiplication. Nonetheless, the idea of gaining time has always been an artistic concern. Andy Warhol once said that any picture that takes more than five minutes to make is a bad picture. And Andy Warhol was also the first one to really grasp the potential of film as a means of exploiting this surplus. His film, *Empire*, was the first step in the development that has led to Fischli/Weiss's videos because it was the first time that the temporal investment in the relationship between artist and viewer was inverted. It used to be that the artist had

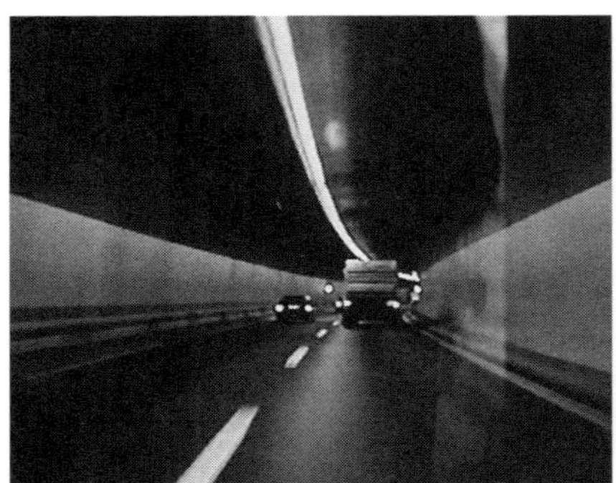

3   Video still from the installation at the Swiss
     Pavilion, Venice Biennale   1995
     color videotape
     Photo: © Mancia/Bodmer

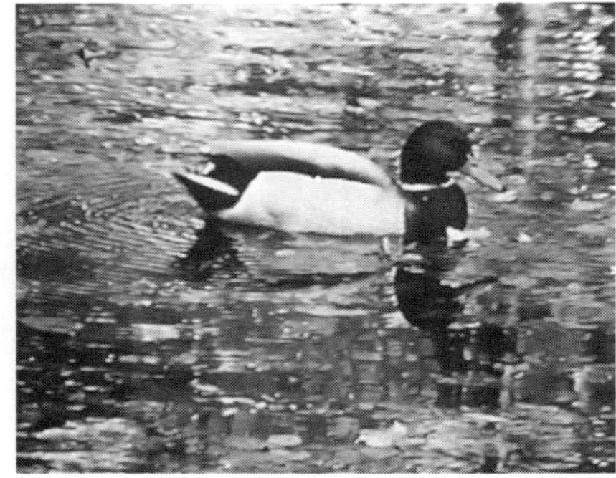

4   Video still from the installation at the Swiss
     Pavilion, Venice Biennale   1995
     color videotape
     Photo: © Mancia/Bodmer

to invest a great deal of time in creating his work, which the viewer was then able to see at one go, so time was apportioned in the viewer's favor but to the artist's disadvantage. And this certainly still applies to art videos that generally take much longer to make than to watch. But *Empire* took exactly the same length of time to make as it does to watch it. Viewers must now invest just as much time in the job of perception as the artists spend in the making of their works. Duchamp already observed that looking at something turns it into a work of art. And as so often happens, the privilege soon became a burden.

In Warhol's case it was not necessary to watch the entire film in order to get the message. After a while the viewer realized that there was more of same, which was basically Warhol's concession to a public accustomed to being able to take in a work of art, if not at a glance, at least within a reasonable length of time. Fischli/Weiss no longer make this concession. The outings recorded in their videos take them from one place to another and could continue anywhere (figures 3–6; pages 63–71). But the videos are anything but monotonous. In some cases they are even suspenseful and startling (animal clinic), beautiful and poetic (mountain landscapes), strange (the army in the mountains, tanks, technoparty), or informative (milking cows, hunting)—but then again banal, same-old-stuff pictures. Where they belong, how important they are, what they mean—these questions can only be answered by surveying the entire enterprise, because Fischli/Weiss have embarked on a journey of discovery through life, whose stations acquire meaning only within the overarching context of the journey as a totality. But two problems arise. First, the artists, like all

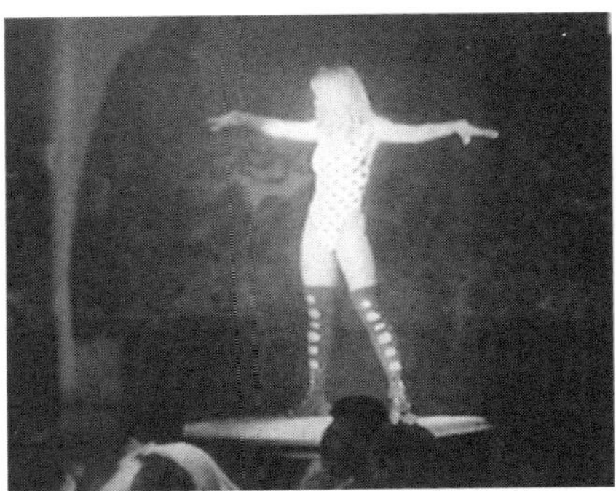

5   Video still from the installation at the Swiss
     Pavilion, Venice Biennale   1995
     color videotape
     Photo: © Mancia/Bodmer

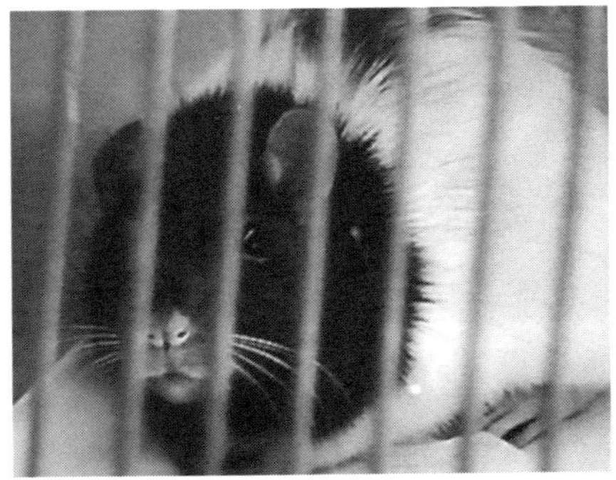

6   Video still from the installation at the Swiss
     Pavilion, Venice Biennale   1995
     color videotape
     Photo: © Mancia/Bodmer

human beings, are finite and mortal, which means that they cannot get a total view. Secondly, it is even harder for viewers because, given the "normal" speed of their lives, there is no way that they will ever be able to catch up with all that the artists have seen and visited.

News reports on television have to be brief, and in the time allotted to them, they have to make a statement that sounds complete. Fischli/Weiss have no such clear-cut ambitions. Their videos are simply an expression of the desire to go out and see if something interesting is happening. This attitude is, of course, out of the question in any professional investigation of an issue of public interest. But Fischli/Weiss show a vague, noncommittal interest in whatever comes their way, which is non-professional and basically a recreational activity, a kind of hobby. It also solves the problem of establishing criteria for selection because, in our spare time, we can devote ourselves to any number of things that are not subject to the censorship of relevance, significance, or innovation.

Now it is most unlikely for average visitors to an exhibition, who would be using their free time to come and look at the work of Fischli/Weiss, to have a supply of time that is large enough to follow the trips Fischli/Weiss took at the same tempo and with undivided attention. Instead they will stop in front of a monitor for a while, and then move on to another one, the end result being that they will have seen only bits and pieces, fragments of the whole, and will be left wondering whether they have seen enough to grasp the overall project. The time relationship between the viewer and the work of Fischli/Weiss is therefore analogous to that between people and life in general. Structurally speaking, human beings are not endowed with enough time to see and understand the whole of life. Similarly, viewers cannot see and understand all the work of Fischli/Weiss because the artists have used the time surplus provided by the speed of contemporary art to put an invisible wall of time between their work and the viewers. It is, of course, conceivable that someone might actually take the time to watch everything Fischli/Weiss have done. It is theoretically possible. But a decision of that nature does not fit in with the conventional conditions of art reception that are still in effect today. Besides, the attempt to watch the entire piece would simply lead to its continuation on the part of the artists because it is basically a work that can never be completed.

In their videos, Fischli/Weiss do not provide viewers with the closure that is their traditional right. Artists are ordinarily expected to give a closed form to a messy and therefore frustrating reality so that it is at least visually consumable. Even if an artistic product is open-ended by design, it can still be grasped and identified at one glance. But in this case, we do not know what the final shape of the work is; perhaps it has a symmetry after all that will not surface unless we watch all of the videos. The work in its entirety escapes not only the viewers' mental but also their physical faculties: it is tiring. Perhaps the most appropriate way to take in this work would be to have the videos at home and watch them day after day as a substitute for daily television, or maybe even as a substitute for daily life.

The readymade procedure involves transporting items of daily life into the domain of the museum. Fischli/Weiss transfer the tempo of leisure and unpressured recreation to their professional lives. And in the process they gain time, twice over. First, they have freed themselves from the professional difficulties that steal time. And secondly, they have extended free time into working time without endangering their jobs. In our society this is a privilege reserved for artists. In return, artists generally feel obliged to show society a compressed and condensed version of what they have seen in all those hours of lonely observation. This is exactly what Fischli/Weiss do, but unabridged.

The difference may not seem very great, but it is decisive. It explains why the work of Fischli/Weiss, so harmless at first sight, is actually merciless. They force viewers to face a shortage of time, in other words, the same situation that they find so frustrating "in real life," that is, the impossibility of taking in all the visual stimuli that present themselves. And this additional frustration happens precisely when viewers expect satisfaction from art. Art has broken many taboos in our century. And all these violations have not only been visible, but have even enhanced the visibility of art. Now, in contrast, a movement is on the rise that is leading art away from visibility. Viewers are increasingly faced with works that withdraw from their gaze, sometimes even more than life itself. Instead of making the invisible visible, which was once considered the traditional task of art, Fischli/Weiss have rendered something perfectly visible — namely, daily Swiss life — invisible because it is hidden away in the length of the videos. Thus banality is becoming mysterious at a time when mystery has faded to banality.

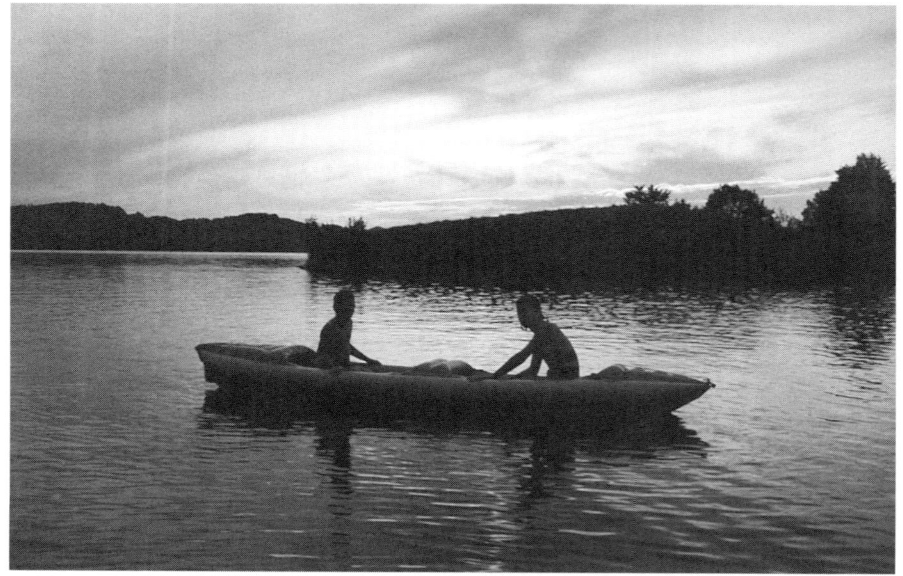

Children in the Boat
from *Bilder, Ansichten (Images, Views)* 1991
Cibachrome

BIOGRAPHY

PETER FISCHLI
Born in 1952, Zürich, Switzerland.
Studied 1975–1976 at the Accademia di
Belle Arti, Urbino, and 1976–1977 at the
Accademia di Belle Arti, Bologna.

DAVID WEISS
Born in 1946, Zürich, Switzerland.
Studied 1963–1964 at the
Kunstgewerbeschule, Zürich,
and 1964–1965 at the
Kunstgewerbeschule, Basel.

The artists live in Zürich, where they
began collaborative work in 1979.

SELECTED SOLO EXHIBITIONS

1981
Galerie Balkon, Geneva
Plötzlich diese Übersicht
  (Suddenly This Overview),
  Galerie Stähli, Zürich

1982
St. Galerie, St. Gallen, Switzerland

1983
Fieber (Fever),
  Monika Sprüth Galerie, Cologne

1984
Galerie Crousel-Hussenot, Paris

1985
Stiller Nachmittag (Quiet Afternoon),
  Monika Sprüth Galerie, Cologne
Kunsthalle Basel / Groninger Museum
Centre Culturel Suisse, Paris
Produzentengalerie, Hamburg
Kunstverein Köln, Cologne

1986
Sonnabend Gallery, New York
The Corridor, Reykjavik

1987
Monika Sprüth Galerie, Cologne
List Visual Arts Center, Massachusetts
  Institute of Technology, Cambridge

(exhibition traveled in 1987–1988
to Renaissance Society, Chicago; Institute
for Art and Urban Resources, P.S. 1,
New York; Museum of Contemporary Art,
Los Angeles; Dallas Museum of Art;
and University Art Museum, Berkeley)
Le Case d'Arte, Milan

1988
Institute of Contemporary Art, London
Third Eye Center, Glasgow
Musée de peinture et de sculpture,
  Grenoble
Interim Art Gallery, London
Portikus, Frankfurt am Main

1989
University of South Florida Art Museum, Tampa
Sonnabend Gallery, New York
Monika Sprüth Galerie, Cologne
Le Case d'Arte, Milan
Galerie Susan Wyss, Zürich
Galerie Akhnaton, Cairo

1990
Galerie Ghislaine Hussenot, Paris
IVAM, Valencia
Kunstverein München, Munich
Galería Marga Paz, Madrid

1991
Kunstverein Düsseldorf
Wiener Sezession, Ausstellunghaus, Vienna
Galerie Achenbach, Frankfurt am Main
Galleria Bonomo, Rome

1992
Musée national d'art moderne, Centre
  Georges Pompidou, Paris
Galleria Locus Solus, Genoa
Galerie Walcheturm, Zürich
Galerie Francesca Pia, Bern

1993
Le Case d'Arte, Milan
Kunsthalle Zürich
Musée d'art et d'histoire, Geneva

1994
Sonnabend Gallery, New York

1995
XLVI Biennale di Venezia, Swiss Pavilion
Monika Sprüth Galerie, Cologne

 SELECTED BIBLIOGRAPHY

BOOKS BY THE ARTISTS

1981
*Ordnung und Reinlichkeit
   (Order and Cleanliness)*,
   Edition by the artists, Zürich

1982
*Plötzlich diese Übersicht
   (Suddenly This Overview)*,
   Edition Stähli, Zürich

1985
*Stiller Nachmittag
   (Quiet Afternoon)*,
   Edition Kunsthalle Basel

*Stiller Nachmittag
   (Quiet Afternoon)*,
   Edition Monika Sprüth Galerie, Cologne,
   and Sonnabend Gallery, New York
   (second edition)

1989
Quiet Afternoon,
   Edition Akhnaton Gallery, Cairo
   (third edition)

Photographs,
   Swiss Federal Office of Culture
   and Edition Patrick Frey, Zürich

1990
Airports,
   Edition Patrick Frey, Zürich,
   and IVAM, Valencia

1991
*Bilder, Ansichten
   (Images, Views)*,
   Edition Patrick Frey, Zürich, and
   Wiener Sezession Ausstellunghaus, Vienna

1993
*Siedlungen, Agglomeration
   (Settlements, Agglomerations)*,
   Edition Patrick Frey, Zürich,
   and Kunsthalle Zürich

1996
*Bericht über den künstlerischen Schmuck
   im Neubau der Börse Zürich
   (Report on the Commission of Works
   in Situ for the New Stock Exchange)*,
   Edition Oktagon Verlag, Stuttgart;
   Hans-Ulrich Obrist, editor

MONOGRAPHS

1981
Bilder (Images),
    Kunstmuseum Winterthur, Switzerland;
    text by Patrick Frey

1985
*Peter Fischli David Weiss: Ein ruheloses
    Universum (A Restless Universe)*,
    Kunsthalle Basel and Groninger Museum;
    texts by Jean-Christophe Ammann
    and Patrick Frey

Peter Fischli, David Weiss,
    Fondation Suisse de la Culture Pro Helvetia,
    Paris; text by Patrick Frey

1987
*Stiller Nachmittag: Aspekte junger
    Schweizer Kunst (Quiet Afternoon:
    Aspects of Young Swiss Art)*,
    Kunsthaus Zürich;
    text by Patrick Frey

Peter Fischli David Weiss,
    List Visual Arts Center, Massachusetts
    Institute of Technology, Cambridge;
    texts by Karen Marta and Patrick Frey

1988
Peter Fischli David Weiss,
    Pro Helvetia Arts Council, Switzerland;
    text by Patrick Frey (expanded version of
    Stiller Nachmittag Kunsthaus Zürich, 1987)

*Fischli et Weiss: Le cours des choses
    (The Way Things Go)*,
    Musée de peinture et de sculpture
    de Grenoble; texts by Serge Lemoine
    and Christine Poullain

Peter Fischli, David Weiss,
    Portikus, Frankfurt am Main;
    text by Patrick Frey

Parkett, no. 17,
    Zürich / New York;
    texts by Bernhard Johannes Blume,
    Germano Celant, Bice Curiger,
    Patrick Frey, Karen Marta,
    Jeanne Silverthorne, and Sidra Stitch

1989
Fischli / Weiss,
    Dallas Museum of Art;
    text by Sue Graze

1990
Die Kunst in der Schweiz (Art in Switzerland),
    Edition Kiepenheuer & Witsch, Cologne;
    text by Robert Fischer

*Das Geheimnis der Arbeit: Texte zum Werk
    von Peter Fischli und David Weiss
    (The Secret of Work: Texts on the Work of
    Peter Fischli and David Weiss)*,
    Kunstverein München, Kunstverein
    Düsseldorf; text by Patrick Frey

1991
Monumente,
    Centre Pasqu Art, Biel, Switzerland;
    text by Andreas Meier

1992
Peter Fischli et David Weiss,
    Musée national d'art moderne,
    Centre Georges Pompidou, Paris;
    texts by Jean-Pierre Bordaz,
    Nicolas Bourriaud, Jean de Loisy,
    Christophe Domino, Patrick Frey,
    Catherine Grenier, Hans-Ulrich Obrist,
    Daniel Soutif, and Katharina Steffen

1994
Parkett, no. 40/41,
    Zürich / New York;
    text by Boris Groys

1995
Peter Fischli David Weiss,
    XLVI Biennale di Venezia, Venice,
    and Bundesamt für Kultur, Bern;
    texts by Bice Curiger, Patrick Frey,
    and Boris Groys

*Peter Fischli/David Weiss, Raum unter
    der Treppe (Room under the Staircase)*,
    Museum für Moderne Kunst, Frankfurt
    am Main, and Cantz Verlag, Stuttgart;
    texts by Jean-Christophe Ammann
    and Rolf Lauter

 # CHECKLISTS

**PETER FISCHLI AND DAVID WEISS:
IN A RESTLESS WORLD**
ORGANIZED BY WALKER ART CENTER

Wurstserie 1979
color photographs 9½ x 13¾ in.
Collection Walker Art Center
Clinton and Della Walker
Acquisition Fund, 1993

    Am Nordpol (At the North Pole)

    Der Brand von Uster (The Fire of Uster)

    Höhlenbewohner (The Caveman)

    Im Teppichladen (In the Carpet Shop)

    In den Bergen (In the Mountains)

    Modeschau (Fashion Show)

    Moonraker

    Pavesi

    Titanic

    Der Unfall (The Accident)

*Plötzlich diese Übersicht
(Suddenly This Overview)* 1981
unfired clay   dimensions vary
Courtesy the artists

    Brot (Bread)

    Discjockey

    *Einheimischer Waldboden
    (Indigenous Forest Floor)*

    *Frau im Supermarkt
    (Woman in the Supermarket)*

    Frau in der Waschküche (Woman in Washroom)

    Garten (Garden)

    Lokomotive (Engine)

    Moderne Siedlung (Modern Development)

    Spanisch Nüsschen (Peanuts)

    Warten auf den Lift (Waiting for the Elevator)

Kleines Bett (Little Bed) 1983
polyurethane, paint   11¹³⁄₁₆ x 21⅝ x 11½ in.
Courtesy the artists

Fragentopf (Question Pot) 1984
polyurethane, cloth, paint   53⅛ x 78¾ x 78¾ in.
Collection Anna Grässlin,
St. Georgen, Switzerland

Röhre (Tube) 1984
polyurethane, cloth, paint   13⅜ x 68½ x 23⅝ in.
Courtesy the artists

Stiller Nachmittag (Quiet Afternoon) 1984–1985
color and black-and-white photographs
dimensions range from 9⅛ x 12 in. to 16 x 12 in.
Courtesy the artists

    Barrikade (Barricade)

    Chinesisches Zeichen (Chinese Symbol)

    Dunkler Trieb (Dark Impulse)

    *Ehre, Mut und Zuversicht
    (Honour, Courage, Confidence)*

    *Flirt, Liebe, Leidenschaft, Hass, Trennung
    (Flirtation, Love, Passion, Hate, Separation)*

    *Frau Birne bringt ihrem Mann vor der Oper ein
    frisch gebügeltes Hemd. Der Bub raucht.
    (Mrs. Pear bringing her husband a freshly ironed
    shirt for the opera. The boy smokes.)*

    Frühe Reife (Early Wisdom)

    Der Furz (The Fart)

    Die Gefahren der Nacht (Night's Dangers)

    Die gefeierte Rübe (The Triumphant Carrot)

    Die Gesetzlosen (Outlaws)

    Hase (Hare)

    Masturbine

    Natürliche Grazie (Natural Grace)

    Ohne Titel (Untitled)

    Ohne Titel (Untitled)

    *Reagans Modell für die bewaffnete Raumfahrt
    (Reagan's Model for Armed Space Travel)*

    Sicheres Auftreten (Aplomb)

    Stiller Nachmittag (Quiet Afternoon)

    Stillstand, Müdigkeit (Standstill, Tiredness)

    Die stolze Köchin (The Proud Cook)

*Unser Leben gleicht der Reise eines
Wandrers durch die Nacht
(Life is like the journey of a traveller
through the night)*

Verfeinerung (Refinement)

Die Verschwörung (The Conspiracy)

Warenhauskönig (Supermarket King)

Der Zorn Gottes (The Wrath of God)

Tier (Animal) 1935
polyurethane, cloth, paint   22 x 38 x 23 in.
Courtesy the artists

Der Lauf der Dinge (The Way Things Go)
1985–1987
16mm color film transferred to laser disc, 30 min.
Courtesy the artists

Surrli 1986
slide projection
Courtesy the artists

Kanalarbeiter (Sewer Workers) 1986
cast rubber, Beracryl   10½ x 18¹¹⁄₁₆ x 7⁷⁄₁₆ in.
Courtesy the artists

Kerze (Candle) 1987
cast rubber, Beracryl   11 x 6⁵⁄₁₆ x 6⁵⁄₁₆ in.
Courtesy the artists

Napf (Dog Dish) 1987
cast rubber, Beracryl   3¾ x 11 in. diam.
Courtesy the artists

Wurzel (Root) 1987
cast rubber, Beracryl   22½ x 18⁵⁄₁₆ x 14½ in.
Collection Kunsthaus Zürich
Vereinigung Zürcher Kunstfreunde
Gruppe junge Kunst

Schallplatte (Record) 1988
cast rubber, Beracryl   4 x 11¹³⁄₁₆ in. diam.
Courtesy the artists

Airports 1988
three Cibachromes   47¼ x 70⅞ in.
Courtesy Sonnabend Gallery, New York

Le rayon vert (The Green Light) 1990
flashlight, turntable, plastic cup, tape
10 x 24 x 10 in.
Courtesy the artists

Airports 1991
Cibachrome   47¼ x 70⅞ in.
Collection Centre Pasqu Art, Biel, Switzerland

Kanalvideo (Canal Video) 1992
color videotape transferred to laser disc, 62 min.
Courtesy the artists

Ohne Titel (Untitled) 1993–1996
polyurethane, paint   dimensions vary
Courtesy the artists

Untitled from the Venice Biennale 1995
30 color videotapes, 80 hours
Courtesy the artists

Ohne Titel (Untitled) 1996
polyurethane, paint   dimensions vary
Courtesy the artists

CHECKLIST FOR THE EXHIBITION
PETER FISCHLI DAVID WEISS
ORGANIZED BY SERPENTINE GALLERY

Surrli 1986
slide projection
Courtesy the artists

Le rayon vert (The Green Light) 1990
flashlight, turntable, plastic cup, tape
10 x 24 x 10 in.
Courtesy the artists

Kanalvideo (Canal Video) 1992
color videotape transferred to laser disc, 62 min.
Courtesy the artists

Untitled from the Venice Biennale 1995
36 color videotapes, 96 hours
Courtesy the artists

Ohne Titel (Untitled) 1995–1996
polyurethane, paint   dimensions vary
Courtesy the artists

PETER FISCHLI AND DAVID WEISS: IN A RESTLESS WORLD

DESIGN **MATT ELLER**
IN COLLABORATION WITH **PETER FISCHLI AND DAVID WEISS**

EDITORS **JANET JENKINS AND KATHLEEN McLEAN**

PUBLICATION MANAGER **MICHELLE PIRANIO**

PHOTOGRAPHS **PETER FISCHLI AND DAVID WEISS** EXCEPT WHERE NOTED

CURATORIAL ASSISTANT **ROCHELLE STEINER**

PRINTED IN THE UNITED STATES OF AMERICA BY
WALLACE CARLSON COMPANY, MINNEAPOLIS

AVAILABLE THROUGH D.A.P./DISTRIBUTED ART PUBLISHERS
636 BROADWAY, 12TH FLOOR, NEW YORK, NEW YORK 10012

REPRODUCTION CREDITS
EXCEPT AS NOTED BELOW, ALL IMAGES ARE COURTESY PETER FISCHLI AND DAVID WEISS.
Hirshhorn Museum and Sculpture Garden, Smithsonian Institution, Washington, D.C.; Photo: Lee Stalsworth: page 106
Rhona Hoffman Gallery, Chicago; Photo: David Reynolds: page 106
Mancia/Bodmer, Zürich: pages 63–69, 92, 118–119
Museum Boymans-van Beuningen, Rotterdam: page 91
The Museum of Modern Art, New York; Photo © David Gahr: page 87
Philadelphia Museum of Art: page 89
Philadelphia Museum of Art; Photo: Graydon Wood: page 109
Ywan Schumacher: pages 1–7, 84, 107
Sonnabend Gallery, New York: page 110
Alex Troehler, Zürich: page 90
The Andy Warhol Foundation, New York: page 109

LIBRARY OF CONGRESS CATALOGING-IN-PUBLICATION DATA PENDING.
LC: 96-12038
ISBN: 0-93540-51-7

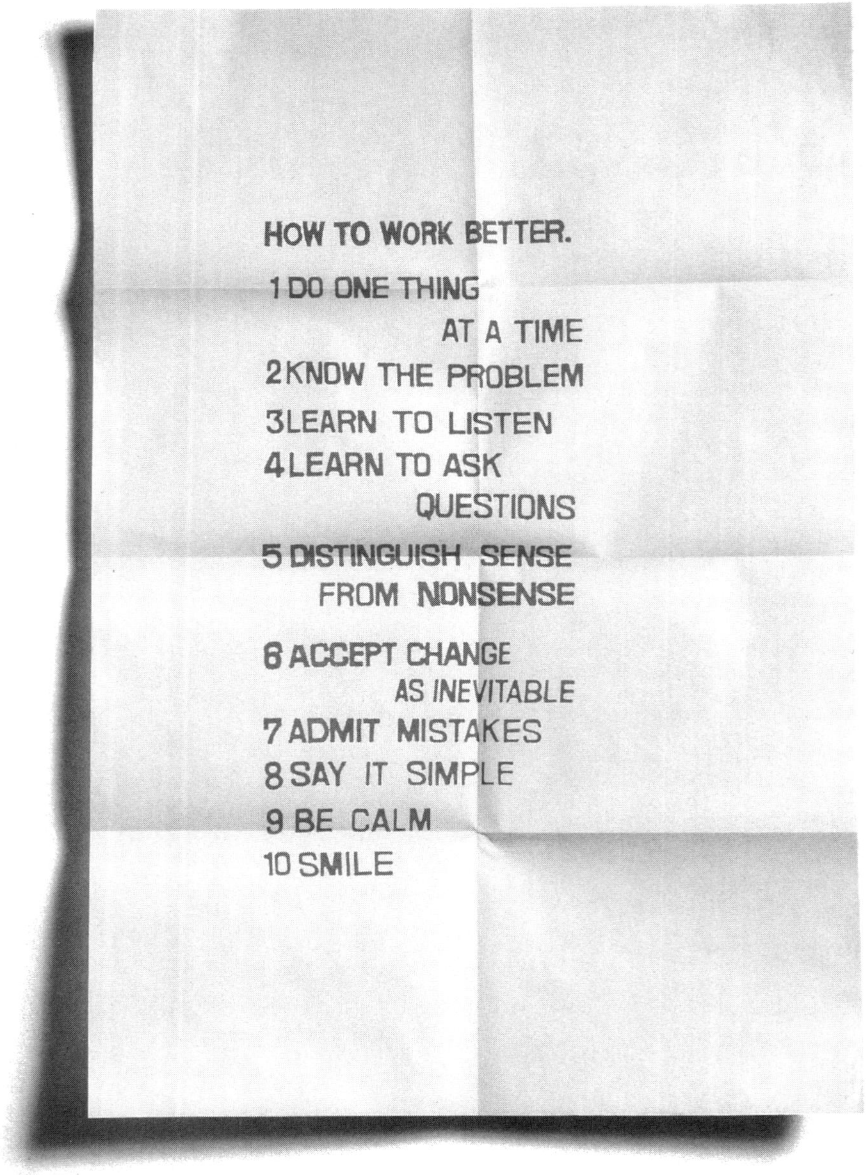

How to Work 1991